Aware

Attentive

'WORSHIP'
IN EVOLVING CHRISTIANITY

JOHN BODYCOMB

First published in Australia in 2012
By Spectrum Publications Pty Ltd
a: PO Box 75, Richmond, Victoria, Australia 3121
t: (+61) 1300 540 736
f: (+61) 1300 540 737
e: spectrum@spectrumpublications.com.au
w: www.spectrumpublications.com.au
for John Bodycomb

© 2012 John Bodycomb
All rights reserved.
No part of this publication may be reproduced
in any manner without prior
written permission of the publisher.

Cover Design: xy arts
Typesetting by Spectrum Publications Pty Ltd
Typeface: Bembo Book, Friz Quadrant

National Library of Australia Cataloguing-in-Publication entry (pbk)

Author: Bodycomb, John, 1931-
Title: Aware and attentive : 'worship' in evolving Christianity /
             John Bodycomb.
ISBN: 9780867861570 (pbk.)
Notes: Includes bibliographical references.
Subjects: God (Christianity)--Worship and love.
             Public worship.
             Christianity--21st century.
Dewey Number: 270.83

GOD IS THE SURROUNDING,
SATURATING SACRED PRESENCE IN
WHOM DWELLS EVERYTHING AND
EVERYONE, WHO INDWELLS EVERYTHING
AND EVERYONE, WHO ENVELOPS AND
INFUSES ALL THAT IS. GOD IS IN ALL AND
ALL IS IN GOD.

(John Bodycomb)

JESUS IS A 'GOD-SOAKED' HUMAN BEING.

(Lorraine Parkinson)

Table of Contents

Introduction

I have written this with some diffidence. It seems to me that there are more than enough mediocre books on some religious topic without my adding one more. But as with other times when I have succumbed to the urge, what motivates this entry into print is a serious disquiet about a serious issue.

Personal spirituality, and my own response to the ineffable mystery we call 'G-O-D' are basic to much of what follows. That is to say, it is about my own journey and also those of others with whom I share reflections. However, this particular exercise is principally about people *worshipping together* – and for those people.

It is very unlikely to gain endorsement from purists – those guardians of the way things are 'meant to be'. But I am inclined these days to believe that the content and form of any activity we call 'worship' are best decided by consensus; *not* by an external authority imposing some particular form on us. Perhaps this is my 'non-conformist' ancestry coming to the fore again! Anyhow, the material consists of short chapters with questions appended to each – making it, I hope, useful for discussion.

Readers of my book *No Fixed Address* (Spectrum Publications 2010) will meet again some of the thinking that was in that, and wonder if I am becoming repetitive in old age. That could always be so, of course, but I hope it is not the case here. There has to be a modest amount of 'recapitulation' here because I cannot assume that all who read this will be familiar with *No Fixed Address*.

Because I want to encourage readers to work out their own ways of worshipping together, I have fought the temptation to set down yet another 'right' way in some recommended order of proceedings! There simply is no single right way to go about this. What I have done is to offer some resources, but that is quite different from telling my readers how things ought to be done! You and only you must decide this.

I am always grateful to those whose intelligence and ideas have enriched mine, and in this work nothing has changed! Specifically, I would acknowledge certain members of my family who are not voracious consumers of religious books, but who rather surprised me by reading *No Fixed Address* and offering comments. There is no predicting such things!

I shall spare their blushes with the exception of my grandson Timothy Wright, currently a Catholic 'in exile'. During a year teaching at a London school Tim read *No Fixed Address* and asked, "If we get to thinking like this, what does it do for the mass &c?" That really set me going.

In putting together this response, I am indebted to several colleagues in 'PEG' (Progressive Explorers Group) and to my wife Dr Lorraine Parkinson, always gentle but firm! Finally, I acknowledge the support and encouragement of Spectrum's Peter Rohr – a friend indeed!

JOHN BODYCOMB
Doncaster, 2012

PART I
RATIONALE

1

Bored Silly!

"He who sits in the heavens laughs; the Lord has them in derision." (Psalm 2:4)

It's an old chestnut, but it may nonetheless have eluded you. It tickles my sense of the ridiculous, any way. Two Aussie tourists were looking at the honour board in a little village church in England. Over the top of twenty or thirty names it had the simple four words: 'died in the service.' One says, "Eh, Bert, my grandson says he's bored to death in church, but I never imagined it could be that bad over 'ere!"

While Chaplain with the University of Melbourne I delivered a lunch-hour series in the Trinity College Chapel on the subject of religion as a laughing matter, and laughing as a religious matter. As a guest preacher at St Michael's (Melbourne) during that time, I also spoke there on the subject. After the service a man wrung my hand at the door. He said, "When I was eight years old, I burst out laughing at something in church. My father took me outside, removed his belt and gave me a whacking in the church porch. You have liberated me to laugh again in church after fifty years!"

My series at the University was called "In the Image of a Smiling God." I have thought about publishing on the subject, but thus far have procrastinated. Let's face it, though. Nothing can be quite so ridiculous as some of the things we do ostensibly in God's name. An Episcopal friend in the US described to me the ordination in a one-time African colony of ten indigenous candidates. A bishop from the Old Country came out to do the honours. Clad in what looked like a brocade bedspread and lacy side curtains, with a corn flakes packet on his head and a big ski pole in one hand, he looked truly majestic, leading in the ordinands. There was no other word for it.

At the steps up to the altar he somehow missed his footing and fell full length. Bits and pieces scattered, and he looked like a heap of washing lying there. With help he picked himself up, rearranged his apparel and took his throne. Immediately upon his doing this, every single one of the ordinands tripped, fell and lay full-length on the steps – believing this to be part of the prescribed liturgy! What is more, story has it that they were still doing ordinations in the same way years later! Probably apocryphal, but it serves to make the point.

Sometimes I think there are few spectacles more absurd than a procession of clergy, wearing what one of my friends calls 'an old man's night shirt', wending their way to the place where they will show off for an hour or so – with fancy posturing and funny voices. And all done with maximum pomp and pretentiousness. We need to be able to stand back occasionally and reflect on what we get up to in the divine name, and be soundly critical of its absurdities. The great Swiss theologian Karl Barth, some of whose devotees are singularly humourless, had a hearty sense of the ridiculous. He was known to joke about pushing his barrow-load of Church Dogmatics around heaven, to the mirth of the angels. They would be too busy singing, he said, to read his 13 volumes!

As I indicated in the Introduction, these musings are about what we variously call 'worship', 'liturgy', 'mass', 'service', 'celebration of faith' or just 'gathering', depending on the tradition to which we belong. It will be a 'first' for me. Although I taught preaching in a theological school and wrote a book on the subject (*Excited to Speak, Exciting to Hear*), I have never written much about worship. So why do it now?

The immediate stimulus is interest provoked by *No Fixed Address: Faith as Journey*. I argued there that in Western society the three 'spires' that have stood atop the Christian edifice are crumbling and tumbling. These I dubbed 'the mythical god-man', 'the singular true faith' and 'the ossified pseudo-science'. Having joined the demolition work, I then turned my attention to reinterpreting Jesus, affirming religious pluralism and proposing a way to think about 'G-O-D' that seems to be more or less congruent with what we know about the history and behaviour of the universe (cosmology). It is rather provocative stuff, but has been enthusiastically received. However, readers admit to being challenged by this recurring question raised for them by *No Fixed Address*. Again and again they say, "OK, if we embrace even *some* of what is in there, what does this mean for what we do when we gather on Sundays (mostly Sundays)? How are we supposed to worship now?"

In the first place, then, what follows here is an attempt to respond respectfully to that sort of question. I cannot say it is an easy exercise. That is why this section is called 'Rationale', laid down this way as much for myself as for you. It is also why I have to begin with a chapter that is brutally honest. The fact is that what we have been doing since time immemorial – more or less without question, seems to have been demonstrably losing its appeal. Even the loyal followers have been complaining. The time for truthfulness about the boredom, and about the banality in much of it, is long overdue.

Stories and jokes about it abound – but are not new. I suspect that almost every reader of this can recall a time when he/she counted the stencils in the dado or on the organ pipes, wagered with a friend on which old pewsitter would fall asleep first, timed the so-called 'long prayer' (that protestant abomination), got into trouble for fidgeting or even for laughing – like that man at St Michael's when I preached about religion as laughing matter and laughing as religious matter.

But the problems are more serious than this. For a start, many who grew up in a church of one sort or another have voted with their feet, and even as I write, more are doing so. The reasons offered are "It's dead boring", "I just don't need it", "It makes no sense to me", "Other stuff takes our time these days", "It insults the intelligence" and so on. Quite simply, there is no longer any wish to be there! It is not just the fact that many have left. Many more have *felt* like leaving – but they have hung in, generally for one of three reasons:
- That is where their friends are,
- Habituated behaviour is not easily changed and
- They are hoping against hope that something good might

come out of it if they can survive long enough.

"I'm about ready to jump", a sixty-eight year old man said to me the other day, "but I'm not *quite* ready. See, I wouldn't know what to put in its place." In the next three chapters I want to look at that statement: what *is* 'the place' of worship?

The odd thing is that we have been so reluctant (or so it would seem) to address these matters honestly. Instead, we go home grumbling to ourselves, maybe to our spouses/partners or close friends – and then next week we go back for more of the same! Even more odd is that clergy (at least in my tradition) can be among the most critical when they are pewsitters. Some of them show little or no interest in finding a place to worship when they are on vacation – and if they do, they can be very hard to please. At one stage, when my wife and I had some free Sundays, we strayed into a few suburban places. It was a sort of ecclesiastical 'pub crawl'. *En route* home from one she said, "Now I think I know why people don't want to go to church!" She had to be a pewsitter to know what it could feel like. So, what are we talking about here? What has been going on?

It is hard to identify one single factor that contributes to pewsitter disapproval or discontent. It may be the earnest but lugubrious presider, whose voice drones and whose tiresome phrases are so predictable. It may be the obligation to stand up and struggle to sing unknown tunes and/or sets of lyrics that look nonsensical. It may be a spatial arrangement that interferes with seeing and hearing clearly what is happening out front; even wretchedly uncomfortable seating. One of my friends actually 'rates' pews; he says you get uncomfortable and fidgety after 15 minutes in some, 30 minutes in others. He will say, "That place has 20-minute pews".

We cannot ignore or excuse the catastrophic decline of preaching, which can be dated from the mid-60s. Sermons (or 'homilies') have never enjoyed the place in Catholic and Anglican churches that they have had in mainline protestant churches, where there was an expectation that the preacher should be scholarly and entertaining. In place of this there came generations who were scholarly and dull, entertaining and trivial, or both dull and trivial – but not worth hearing! Many preachers these days seem to think that they are born orators who need no preparation, or they think that the Holy Spirit is a labour-saving device. Observations on the poor standard of preaching are heard commonly today. Some try to justify this by saying that preaching is a relic of former times. I have news for them!

Dismissal of preaching as ineffectual or passé is absurd when one of the fastest growing industries is the monologue at conferences, conventions, seminars and dinners – generally for a fee of $3,000 upwards. Many on the circuit are thought to be worth that and more, for a product that is entertaining, inspiring and motivational. When I was dean (1977-1986) of the Uniting Church's theological school in Melbourne, students grew accustomed to my little signs in unexpected places that said "Boredom is the ultimate blasphemy." Behind that was my admonition, "Bore me in your own name if you must, but to bore me in the divine name is the ultimate blasphemy – for there could never be anything dull about the One who dreamed up this universe." Enough on deficient preaching.

Wherever there are Christians, there is 'worship' of some sort. Whilst certain features are held in common by all traditions, there is also a huge variety of styles. These range from the most simple and plain to the most ornate and mysterious; compare a circle of Quakers sitting in silence, and an Orthodox congregation surrounded by smoke and icons, with their priest half-singing and half-intoning in a form of Greek that only he understands! Or compare a dignified conservative liturgy at your place with the ear-splitting band, swaying congregation and wound-up preacher in that revival centre down the road. I believe there are still some places in the U.S. where they go in for snake-handling, although I have never seen it. But having said all this,

- We seldom analyse what we think we're trying to do.
- We seldom assess whether it's doing whatever it should be doing.
- We seldom attempt research that might suggest changes.
- We seldom venture far afield – lest somebody be upset.

Apart from grumbling to ourselves and our spouses (if we have them) en route home, we seldom address any of the foregoing. It is a rare local congregation or parish that has a worship committee.

Even rarer to have a group that sits down to examine material like this book – with an eye to maybe discovering something new.

Meanwhile the disaffected continue dropping out quietly, to avoid further distress and anger. One of my friends who is a well known figure in Catholic educational circles, working with adults interested in 'spirituality', says she does not encourage them to go to mass – because it has done them too much emotional harm!

Perhaps, until one knows the experience not just of being bored silly, but even downright infuriated, there will not be much progress in this department – and then maybe it will be too late.

QUESTIONS FOR THOUGHT AND TALK

1. Can you recall a 'worship' occasion that was memorable – for good reasons? What made it so for you?

2. What are some of the aspects of 'worship' lately that you have found unappealing – or even thoroughly distasteful?

2

Whence 'Aware and Attentive'?

*"Whoever would approach him must believe that he
exists and that he rewards those who seek him"
(Hebrews 11:6)*

No Fixed Address (2010) is sub-titled 'Faith as Journey'. That is because
I see being a faith person as a constant journey of discovery, in which
one never finally 'arrives'. The book was ten years in the writing but
was all of seventy-nine in formation (I was born in 1931). It was my
way of dealing with three very troublesome issues for a lot of Western
Christians; namely,

- Who Jesus is in the 21st century – especially if we no longer
  cling to the notion that he is somehow 'divine';
- What it means to be faithful to Christianity in a religiously
  'pluralist' world;
- What 'G-O-D' means in a cosmos where we are seven
  million miles from where we were this time last week (at the
  rate at which the universe is expanding)!

Some would consider *No Fixed Address* heterodox if not downright
heretical. But it was not written for those who consider themselves
the guardians of correct thinking. It was written for those who have
been grappling with these questions (above), and not getting what
they would consider helpful answers. There are many such individuals
hanging in churches by the skin of their teeth, as there are also many
more who have given up. For instance, it is my clear impression that
as many as 70 to 80 percent of these folk could be closet 'unitarians'.
(Consult your dictionary if you do not know what that is)

The work is also for my fellow clergy, many of whom find the traditional formulations of faith making less and less sense to them. This may explain in part why some preaching is so dispassionate and unconvincing; they simply don't believe what they think they are expected to believe. How do I know? In more than fifty years of talking privately with clergy of many origins – ostensibly victims of over-work, burn-out and break-down, I have found *the single major factor to be these unacknowledged problems of belief!*

In writing *No Fixed Address* I came to a deeper appreciation of the way everyone is the product of a story. In every case that story spans at least the term of one's own life, but it also includes one's ancestry; many generations of it! This helps to explain why no two persons can ever be identical; each is the product of a different story. It also helps to explain why no two persons can ever think exactly the same way about big subjects like the meaning of faith and hope and love – and G-O-D! Of course, there will be similarities, and these are often enhanced by our exchanging insights and opinions – but identical thinking? No, that is a nonsense.

This realisation, which has taken a while for me to see as clearly as I do today, is very important to my accepting why *your* ideas may be so different from mine. But it is a reminder also that in sharing my own perspectives on subjects like those I've mentioned, it is important for me to try to explain their origin; in other words, to tell a bit of the story. For this reason the first part of *No Fixed Address* was an account of formative experiences and 'defining moments' that I saw as helping to account for the way I am, and for the way I think. I felt that I owed that much to my readers. I feel the same way about sharing reflections in this present work on what we call 'worship' – whatever that is.

The fact is that my own experience of what I call 'G-O-D' has been constantly changing and (I hope) getting richer and deeper with time. I realise that it may well have begun in the womb, with my pregnant mother softly humming her favourite hymn, but that is not accessible to conscious memory. However, let me share with you what I *do* recall, beginning with the strange consequence of a major epidemic.

In the 1930s and 40s somewhere between 2 and 4 million Australians are thought to have contracted the polio virus, and between 20 and 40 thousand were left with some effects. In the worst cases this was paralysis. The advent of powerful vaccines, followed by mass immunisation, has since removed the threat of polio, of course, although we must remain on our guard against a recurrence. But when I was a boy in the 1930s polio was a frightening presence. Mother would point to these huge wicker prams on high wheels, bearing kids my age lying flat and looking forlorn. Some people gave them a wide berth. Mother would say, "They have infantile paralysis, John." She later told me that I had in fact been a suspect – manifesting the signs but fortunately without paralysis.

I gather it was this that helped to tip the scale in my parents' decision to enrol me at the nearby O'Neill College, Gardenvale, run by the Presentation Sisters of the Catholic Church. It could be said that a polio epidemic helped to shape my faith and life! Mother and Dad agreed that I should take part in the school's religious life, and the sisters said (tongue in cheek, I suspect) that they would not try to make me a Catholic! Besides the crucifix in our classroom, prayers each morning and the requirement that we write 'AMDG' *(Ad Majoram Dei Gloriam)* on every page of our work, we trooped each week into the chapel. No explanation was given; we just did it.

I have the clearest record of these times. The sisters wore full black habit, with only faces and hands visible. They were girt by strings of black beads (rosaries) that rattled as they walked among us. The only other sound was that of their rubber soles squishing on the floor. Embedded in my brain is the heady aroma of the enveloping incense. In favourable conditions, I can still call up that olfactory sensation. I was aware of something that was beyond sight and sound, beyond definition or explanation, but eminently and powerfully real. At the time I had no words for it; certainly no godtalk vocabulary.

Now, fast forward twelve or thirteen years. Whatever I had met in chapel at O'Neill College was back in my life. The experience was rather like falling in love – in the sense that it wasn't particularly 'rational'. But it was full of primal energy and enthusiasm. (By the way, 'enthusiasm' comes from the Greek *en theos,* which means 'in

God') In that old expression, I was 'converted'. The community in which this took place would have shied away from a term like 'mystical', but in fact it suited quite well. They had grown out of the so-called 'Oxford Group' movement of the 1920s and 30s, and they put a premium on the daily quiet time. This was a spiritual practice that was principally about what we called seeking 'guidance'. In other words, prayer was pre-eminently an exercise in *listening*: paying attention to what I have called the 'holy whispers'.

For years, until I was married with small children (who tend to upset one's prayer life), I would rise early and sit for half-an-hour on the floor in a kind of modified lotus position – elbows resting on knees and head in hands. It was more easily done and more comfortable then than I find it today! In this position I would try to clear my head of the noises competing for attention, and give my attention to the Mystery around and within.

It was easy back then to think that one had a hot line to heaven, and that just about anything that came into our heads was 'guidance' from God! Warning: beware invoking the divine name as justification for something you want to do! Looking back from where I am now, it was perhaps all a bit 'precious', but I believe the quiet time was (and *is*) a good discipline. Whereas the first marker in my journey could be called *awareness* (as in the chapel at O'Neill College), I guess an appropriate word for this stage might be *attentiveness*.

I tried to preserve this practice as long as I could, but inevitably the demands of family, household tasks and obsession with 'getting stuff done' (compulsive clergy disorder) won out. Also, this stage would have overlapped with periods of major questioning in matters of faith and theology, when for a time I didn't feel too much like praying. I tended to content myself with corporate religious life – hoping that if 'G-O-D' had something to tell me, it would filter through.

My interest in meditative practices was reignited in the late 60s, when I worked under considerable pressure – as both full-time post-graduate student and full-time village parson in the USA. It was in Boston that I met Thich Nhat Hanh, the renowned Vietnamese Buddhist monk and tireless peace activist. Like the Dalai Lama, Thich

Nhat Hanh had achieved an exquisite harmony between the interior life and activism – which I have always coveted and never achieved!

Then back in Australia I encountered the teachings of Sri Chinmoy (1931-2007). He was a Bengali mystic (Hindu) who settled in 1964 in the USA, where he had been summoned by men and women who were unsatisfied with Christian spirituality. Sri Chinmoy's haunting flute music was at the time a powerful non-verbal aid to meditation. Latterly I have also drawn on the shakuhachi music of Riley Lee, a U.S. born Australian and grand master of shakuhachi. Shakuhachi is the traditional bamboo flute, end-blown, used by Zen Buddhist monks in meditation, and I find Riley Lee's music particularly conducive to a mood of attentiveness.

I have become less and less enamoured of the florid barrage of words often presented as 'prayer' (especially in my own tradition), and privately have moved closer to non-verbal meditative practices. I do not dismiss 'saying' prayers (including aloud) and will return to this in Chapters 11 and 12. I return also to the significance of music, and specifically of the flute as a religious 'icon', in Chapter 9.

Today *Awareness* and *Attentiveness* are for me the two major 'motifs' in any spiritual practice – either solo or together in community. Hence the title of this book! But I also have my daily 'labyrinth' – although it is not strictly a labyrinth. (Not to be confused with a maze, a labyrinth is a circuitous path one walks thoughtfully, and which symbolises a journey of going into the centre of oneself.) With rare exceptions when I have been aboard a plane, I have walked 3.25km early every morning for the last fifteen years. Weather and darkness do not present problems. My 'labyrinth' is a huge nearby sports oval, which I circle four times. I pursue exactly the same route, diverted only by birds or the occasional human with whom one exchanges a polite nod. My eyes are fixed on the ground 2-3 metres ahead of me.

Into the first lap, I find my mind emptying. Often I have a sense of connectedness with the ground, as bearing me up on its velvety green carpet. I register this sense of oneness with my home planet, beyond it with the universe, and in all of this with 'G-O-D'. Who is this of whom I speak? As the fly leaf has it, God is for me the surrounding, saturating sacred presence in whom dwells everything and everyone, who indwells everything and everyone, who envelops and infuses all that is. For me, unashamedly 'panentheist', God is in all and all is in God. It is rare for me to have what I would regard as a conscious 'exchange' with the Eternal One, although later I shall recount something that seemed like it.

This is the tale of my own spiritual formation up to the present, a process that I expect to continue – because I have 'no fixed address'! It is necessary to help explain why I feel at home in a Quaker meeting house, and often wish for a more serious use of *silence* in worship than those ridiculous little five-second breathers! It may help explain why I feel less and less at home in the deluge of religious gobbledegook that one meets most Sundays in church! I am asking "Is this the best way to 'worship'?"

Before leaping into that question too precipitately, it is necessary to explore a teasing question; namely, 'Are we, in fact, somehow 'hard-wired'?' Could Awareness and Attentiveness be somehow quite natural?

QUESTIONS FOR THOUGHT AND TALK

1. Where and when would you say that you've had a sense of the 'really real-ness' of God?

2. Do you pursue any regular 'spiritual practice' because you find it's good for you?

3

Are we somehow 'hard-wired'?

"So God created humankind in his image, in the image of God he created them; male and female he created them." (Genesis 1:27)

In 1952 I entered theological school in Melbourne, and in that first year was required to read Rudolf Otto's *The Idea of the Holy* (first published 1917). Otto (1869-1937) had taught at the University of Breslau and then at the University of Marburg's Divinity School, where he stayed until retirement. His most famous work (in German *Das Heilige*)★ has never been out of print!

Rudolf Otto wrote about what he called 'the sense of the numinous'. He derived this word from the Latin *numen* (deity). The numinous is a mystery (Latin *mysterium*) that is both overwhelming (*tremendum*) and fascinating (*fascinans*). It seemed to me that Otto was describing to a tee what I had registered as a small boy in the chapel at O'Neill College. It all came back to me.

But why this experience – and not some other? Why this memory – and not some other? Why *any* experience at all? Why could I not have remained unaffected (even bored silly) by those chapel visits? The short answer is that I was somehow *ready* to respond in certain ways to certain stimuli. Never mind whether there is a deity or not; nor whether this kind of experience suggests (much less proves) the existence of a deity. It may be considered some kind of evidence, but that is not the same as proof. And it is not the point here. The point is that I had some sort of built-in equipment for this sense of the 'numinous', as Otto called it. Otherwise it would not have happened.

These days we call the experiences I describe 'awe', 'wonder', 'reverence' or a blend of all these. My point is that the *capacity* for this experience had to be in me before ever I had any theology or any Christian vocabulary to describe or interpret it – much less to explain it. Could this be explained, therefore, by saying that I was somehow 'hard-wired' for it (even genetically programmed, if you wish)?

Fast forward again, to 1989. This was the year I met Manfred Clynes (b.1925), and was flung totally unprepared into a foreign land called 'neurophysiology'. To explain how this happened, I need to say who Manfred Clynes is. In the 1930s and 40s he had been a teenage inventor and piano prodigy in Australia before graduating from the University of Melbourne at 21 with degrees in engineering science and music. At the same time he received a three-year fellowship at the Juilliard School of Music in USA.

Back in Australia after studying under the world's best, Clynes performed as a concert pianist to huge acclaim. Then he returned to the USA, this time to study the *psychology* of music. He became a close friend of Albert Einstein, whose commendation brought him a triumphant concert tour of Europe. He went on to combine study of brain activity with regular concert performances.

In 1989 and now retired, Clynes was a professorial associate in the psychology department at the University of Melbourne and living at Queens College – which is where I met him. The first occasion was a soirée in the senior common room, where he announced a composition unknown to me, by a composer unknown to me. He then took his place at a concert grand and played for 30–35 minutes without any music in front of him. Through this performance I experienced surges of every major emotion in my repertoire, and felt a mixture of both exhaustion and exhilaration at its conclusion.

There would be no surprises in this for the student of music history, who would recognise what has been called 'the doctrine of affections'. In the 17th and 18th centuries there was a widely held belief that the main aim of music was to arouse the passions or affections. In fact, music was compared with rhetoric for its power to evoke such responses. Manfred Clynes knew from his experience as a musician how various kinds of music drew an answering chord in the hearer.

When I told him of my experience while he played, he first admitted that both composition and composer were fictitious, that he had made up the music, and that he was not surprised at the effect on me. All this was intended! Now fascinated, I asked if I might visit him to discuss further what had happened – not just to me but to the others at the soirée. There followed several chats, where we met in his quarters at Queens College.

In the first of these he set about explaining what he had discovered about patterns of brain activity in certain basic emotional states. For seventeen years he had been chief research scientist, and director of the biocybernetics laboratories at Rockland State Hospital in Orangeburg, N.Y. The substance of his work on the nature of emotions can be found in *Sentics: The Touch of the Emotions*, first released in 1977.

The 'sentic states' (from Latin *sentire*, to feel) on which he had concentrated were seven; viz., anger, hate, grief, love, sex, joy and *reverence!* He also studied hope, courage, guilt and shame, and made the point that this repertoire was by no means exhaustive. Naturally, I asked, "But why the first seven?" Not surprisingly, he explained by saying that these were contagious, communicable and often conveyed in and/or stimulated by music. Hence his focus on them. His friend Yehudi Menuhin (1916-99), the renowned violinist, wrote in a foreword to *Sentics*,

> "It is obvious that this signal breakthrough could only have been achieved by a musician. Dr Clynes is a very distinguished pianist; a scientist who remains a musician at heart."

He charted precise physiological expressions of each sentic state, and found a quite remarkable consistency across cultures! His conclusion was that these were not 'learned' (as we pick up from others ways of acting); they were of our very nature!

> "Precise, genetically programmed brain processes have been found to exist which determine the way we perceive and express emotions."

All this may sound a bit technical if not downright boring. You may even wish to question his research method; certainly much more work has been done in the area over the past three decades. However, I am persuaded of Professor Clynes' good faith and the quality of his research at the time it was done. Moreover, I find it profoundly important to our consideration of worship. In a word, what Manfred Clynes argued from his research was that we are somehow 'hard-wired' *inter alia* for reverence!

That is to say, whether there is a deity or not (a matter I leave for the moment), he contended that *reverence* is as natural for us as anger, hate, grief, love, sex and joy – and just as appropriate! This helps to explain why at the age of seven I had that child-level experience of the 'numinous' in chapel at O'Neill College. Before we go any further, note one more thing about this 'sentic state' of *reverence*. Manfred Clynes found that it could be very good for us!

> *"Effort tends to disappear. Rather, there is a sense of receiving and of participation in the larger creative process – paradoxically it makes a person feel both insignificant and secure, and also strong in a way that, unsought, becomes an antidote to depression."*

I thought of Augustine's oft-quoted statement: "Thou hast made us for thyself, and our hearts are restless 'til they rest in thee." And I thought of times and places where I had been 'replenished'. Almost invariably these have been when a profound reverence was evoked, almost always by music. And I thought 'what ever is worship about – if it is not to help us express this built-in tendency?'

I also found myself asking 'if this is in everyone, why do so few find suitable opportunity for its expression in churches?' Worse still – why do I register this so infrequently in church? My mind goes back to the words that appeared each semester at the University of Melbourne on fliers advertising my lunch-hour services, when I was chaplain there.

> *"Worship is both the highest and the healthiest activity in which human beings can engage. To get one's mind off oneself and focussed upon the sacred, opens the way for dramatic changes in one's life."*

Manfred Clynes was a pioneer contributor to the question asked in this chapter, but he was by no means the last. A decade or so after

I met him, Andrew Newberg and Eugene D'Aquili (Univ of Pennsylvania) were releasing results from their research on brain function in persons meditating. Their book *Why God Won't Go Away* (2002) neither confirms nor refutes the existence of deity; it affirms only that we seem be 'hard-wired' for awareness of something we commonly call God.

This delivered the new word – 'neurotheology'. Sceptics, opposed to religion, seized on this to argue that religious experience should be seen just as a biologically determined good feeling, and that there was no ultimate reality (G-O-D) behind it. However, Newberg and D'Aquili were at pains to emphasise that they were not out to establish the existence or non-existence of God; they were simply studying brain function!

Canadian neuroscientist Mario Beauregard and science writer Denyse O'Leary have dared to go further than this in *The Spiritual Brain: A Neuroscientist's Case for the Existence of the Soul* (2007). Based on research with Carmelite nuns, Beauregard warns against explaining away religious experience as a mere artifact of the brain, as neural pathology or as an evolutionary idiosyncrasy. O'Leary reminds us that Paul the Apostle, Joan of Arc, Teresa of Avila and Thérèse of Lisieux were all thought to be epileptics!

Some of the definitive work in this area has continued under the direction of Boston University's Patrick McNamara, an associate professor of neurology. McNamara has edited a three-volume series on religion and the brain, *Where God and Science Meet*, and more recently has published *The Neuroscience of Religious Experience*. In the preface to this work he makes the powerful claim that

> *"Religion is a defining mark of humanity – as emblematic of its bearer as the web for the spider, the dam for the beaver, and the song for the bird."*

Put very simply, as with all the others I cite, McNamara finds that the religious 'tendency' is a universal feature of human nature, which has evolved because it enables us to live better than we would without it! I am not at all troubled by these theories; on the contrary, I find them both illuminating and reinforcing. If such a disposition *is* the product of evolution, as Manfred Clynes observed to me some twenty-three years ago, this surely is because it has some 'survival' value – which in my judgement makes it a good thing! Indeed, although a rabid atheist, even Richard Dawkins believes there could be some evolutionary advantage not to believing in God, but in having the kind of brain that *can* believe in God! There is a difference – at least for Dawkins. The teasing question, of course, is not why some people are more plainly religious than others – but why so many appear to deny something that would seem to be part of their essential nature!

I conclude this section on whether we are somehow 'hard-wired' with the following story. In 1992 my late wife Mavis and I took the grand tour of Europe, rocketing through eight countries in three weeks. A good judge of non-verbal signals, she correctly read some of the French as being rather off-handed with us. I pointed out that our massive coach was emblazoned in metre-high script with the name of that Spanish coast where Nelson had routed the combined French and Spanish fleets – 'Trafalgar Tours'! If I were French, I might consider that somewhat provocative.

Although generally similar in age and ethnicity, coach tourists are in other ways fascinatingly variegated. One learns with whom to engage and whom to evade. Among the latter was a noisy middle-aged pair with a couple of noisome teenage kids. He in particular was given to offering opinions (unsought) on everything. When he extracted from me my occupation, that meant religion was in the frame; he was clearly hostile to it and I could see that he was out to provoke me. There were regular swipes.

Hence I was more than a trifle surprised when we paused at one of the big churches and after a short while inside, my sceptical friend dropped to his knees for several minutes. As we left the place, he wore a different expression. "Some place, eh?" I said. "Something in there I can't account for", he mumbled as he walked alone across to our coach. For just a few moments he had been lost in another kind of *awareness*.

It is this sort of vignette that prompts the question "Are we somehow 'hard-wired' for awe, wonder, reverence – or something of the sort?" Not necessarily hard-wired for G-O-D. That would be a theological question. A sceptic dropping to his knees in a cathedral does not prove the existence of anything, but it does raise the question of whether there is something in our make-up that makes the expression of awe, wonder, reverence (or however you wish to put it) somehow natural.

Could it be natural to all of us, even if it gets to be widely mislaid or repressed? And, of course, it could well be one of those 'hieroglyphs of the heart' (as I call them in *No Fixed Address*), pointing to the Eternal Mystery, but that can remain a matter of opinion here.

QUESTIONS FOR THOUGHT AND TALK

1. Does research like that of Clynes, Newberg and D'Aquili, *et al*, upset your faith or help it?

2. Do you think the 'wiring' for reverence could indeed be in everyone? Why, then, so little evidence of it?

* **Full title:** *Das Heilige – Über das Irrationale in der Idee des Göttlichen und sein Verhältnis zum Rationalen (The Holy – On the Irrational in the Idea of the Divine and its Relation to the Rational)*

4

Dyb, dyb, dyb! Dob, dob, dob!

*"They devoted themselves to the apostles' teaching
and fellowship, to the breaking of bread and the
prayers." (Acts 2:42)*

Remember "Dyb, dyb, dyb. Dob, dob, dob"? You should if you were in cubs or were a cub leader. When my son David (b 1957) was in cubs, meetings began with a leader calling out "Dyb, dyb, dyb" (Do your best) and the pack shouting back "We'll dob, dob, dob" (We'll do our best). The call is heard less often these days. But in David's day it was a very important cub 'ritual'.

Also in those days, the leader had an interesting way of keeping the pack together if they were on an excursion to beach, zoo or some other attraction. With her charges standing to attention in a huddle, she would have one boy hold the end of a length of rope. She would pass this around the pack until back where she started, and then knot it (a reef knot, of course!) Each boy held the encircling loop. The effect was to make what I call for the purpose of this chapter 'a coherent and purposeful whole' – out of a gaggle of small boys who might otherwise scatter, get lost or fall under a truck!

This struck me at the time as a useful metaphor for the collective function of good religion. That word is thought to come from the Latin *ligare*, 'to bind' or *re-ligare*, 'to bind again what was apart'. Good religion as a socially bonding agent helps to make out of a collection of people what you might call 'a coherent and purposeful whole'.

But also, in an individual sense good religion can be the key to personal 'integration'. Where I might otherwise fly into pieces (at worst, 'disintegrate'), good religion can make of my own life a coherent and purposeful whole. Note how we sometimes say of someone "She's got it all together" or alternatively "He's coming apart."

Chapter 2 (Whence 'Aware and Attentive'?) was fairly subjective in its focus on personal experience. Chapter 3 (Are we Somehow 'Hard-wired?') was somewhat scientific. This chapter is different again, drawing on sociology – social theory, and it relies on stories because I like to tell stories!

In the 1960s I was minister with a congregation in New Hampshire (USA). My proposal to church council that the Bible be borne in ahead of my entry on Sunday mornings met with approval, and then came the first occasion for this. Processing out after the service, I was stopped in my tracks by Emmons Sanborn, lead bass in the choir. Em was looking decidedly cross. He barked at me, "We don't want none of that *damn* ritual here, parson!" Those were his exact words.

My astonishment at his tone can be understood if I explain that the service was a classic Nonconformist 'hymn sandwich': four hymns, two readings, offering, three prayers, anthem and 18 minute sermon: every time exactly the same except for Communion Sunday! But there is more. Immediately before the service an acolyte in white surplice would enter by the left-side aisle, light two candles on the altar (yes, an 'altar') and exit by the right-side aisle. Then the choir, resplendent in green and gold gowns, would process in. The minister wore black cassock and clerical collar, preaching gown and so-called 'Geneva bands' – those little white tabs beneath his collar. He processed in last, while the troops stood.

I said, "Emmons, *everything* we do here on Sunday is 'ritual'!" It was, too – as are many of the things that we do in daily life. With any ritual there was always a first time, of course, but then we repeat the process over and over, and the way we do it becomes somehow important in itself. Often it makes little or no sense to the outsider – like the way my family always sing 'happy birthday', deliberately off-key! Never mind the explanation of that.

So, before we rush too quickly into defining 'worship' after chapters 2 and 3, and making a shopping-list of what should go into it, I want to suggest this little excursion into cultural anthropology or sociology, and consider something very important that this tells us about human beings in society: specifically on the place of what are sometimes called by the technical terms 'ritual' and 'myth' – although I propose to ditch those words for what I think are better alternatives. I suggest we go for 'ceremony' and 'story'. That is because critics of dull and mechanical worship sometimes use 'ritual' as a pejorative term to denote something dull and mechanical. 'Myth' (which actually means something like sacred story) is thought by many to denote a furphy, a fallacy, a fantasy – definitely untrue!

In fact, we live as neighbours with guardians of one of the world's greatest treasuries of ceremony and story, with its attendant art work. On a recent visit to Western Australia I was privileged to attend the opening of an exhibition from the estate of the late Mabel King (1938-2006), distinguished aboriginal painter from the Mowanjum people. Her works depict the Wandjina, cloud and rain spirits. Commonly they are depicted with large upper bodies and heads that show eyes and nose, but no mouths. Like religious icons in Christian tradition, Wandjina paintings are treated with great respect. They evoke a sense of awe, wonder and reverence in the viewer.

This is what ceremony and story are all about. Four points to ponder about 'ceremony' (or what the social scientist would call ritual)

- Human beings are creatures of 'ceremony'; that is, customary actions that help to bond us together. Birthday parties and other family events come to mind.
- These ceremonies are often 'celebrative' of beliefs and values that are held in common and are thought to be worth keeping alive.
- They have a reinforcing effect on those who practise them; the beliefs and values are strengthened and so are the people.
- Ceremonies can be solitary (as in private devotions), but commonly are corporate.

Alongside ceremony, the other great bonding agent is myth (or story). 'Myth' is a technical word that comes from the Greek word *mythos*, which means a poetic or legendary story – as distinct from a strictly historical account. That is to say (and I hate labouring the point!), the precise historical accuracy of every minor detail is less important than the 'truth' or 'truths' that come wrapped in this story. 'Myth' in social sciences means a story that wraps the central beliefs that define and animate and guide a company of people. Marcus Borg uses the term 'symbolic narrative'; that is, as distinct from any strictly historical account.

Let me illustrate with an example of how ceremony, story (and holy icon!) work. Remember, the power of all this does not stand on the precise historical accuracy of every minor detail! This is the case of the Bandywallop Football Club. The story *(myth)* comes out of a legendary grand final in 1908. Bandywallop, with only fourteen of its eighteen-man side on their feet by the last quarter, came from behind and in the closing eight minutes overtook Gunns Gully to take out the premiership. Ten of the Bandywallop men never played again. No wonder! Five of them were in their forties and one was fifty-six. One chap actually died from injuries sustained in the match!

Such is the story, any way. In the dressing room at Bandywallop there is one of those old footy tops they wore back then, a faded photograph of the 1908 team, and beside it in a frame the words of the club song. The words are quaint and quirky and they do not rhyme very well, but they are sung before every game as the boys link arms in the dressing room, and then stand mute and motionless for one minute remembering past heroes. This ceremony (ritual) involves a symbolic story (myth?), hero figures, a song, physical actions and a special gathering place. Does it sound like anything else that we do – say on Sundays?

All this ceremony and story serves two essential purposes. One is the bonding of the players. The other, of course, is a reminder of who they are, their *raison d'être*. From a sociological perspective, this is always the purpose of stories and ceremonies (myths and rituals) in any social group – including the family, of course. Pity help anyone who messes around with the tradition! One coach tried to fix some infelicities in the Bandywallop club song, and was threatened with the sack. You see, it is deeply 'religious' stuff for these chaps!

Now, allow me to leap ahead with a brief application of this theory to what we do on Sundays. Worship is a package of story and ceremony. The story and ceremony are what bind us together and make of us a *cohesive and purposeful whole*. (Remember those words?) The story and custom are crucial to our identity and to our continuity; to our *raison d'être*, if you like. Mess with this and we won't know who we are any more!

The story and the ceremony are all about this utterly mysterious One we dare to name, who is the ground of all that is – the One in whom we live and move and have our being, as Paul puts it (Acts 17:28). They are also about the peerless Guru from the Galilee: about his life and his teachings on the art of living. The late Arthur Peacocke (1924-2006), Anglican priest and professor of biochemistry at Oxford, called him the 'God-informed person *par excellence*', whose wisdom seems to have a kind of 'transcendent' quality. My wife Lorraine Parkinson calls him 'God-soaked' and I have taken this over from her.

We also have our customary (ritual!) ways of hearing and reflecting on the stories. Hymns, prayers, homilies and practices like the 'eucharist' are all meant to be part of the way we are reminded of who we are. Our togetherness is to signify that we are part of a movement that was originally called 'the Way'.

Remember, before ever there was a church, or any Christian scriptures, or any creeds or any clergy, there was a *movement* of some kind gathered around this supremely enlightened person who invited others to be similarly enlightened. The ideas that give Christians their reason for being, their mission, their ethic and their 'style' come from him – or should come from him! So it was that Luke should write of those early followers,

> *"They devoted themselves to the apostles' teaching and fellowship,
> to the breaking of bread and the prayers."* (Acts 2:42)

Whatever we eventually decide 'worship' is, and how we want to go about it, this will involve both content and packaging; that is, both story and ceremony. Maybe sacred icons too! We are setting out in *Aware and Attentive* to find the best of story and ceremony for Evolving Christianity. In the next chapter we explore first what so-called 'Evolving Christianity' is about, and then at what might go into the way we celebrate this together.

QUESTIONS FOR THOUGHT AND TALK

1. Can you list some repeated actions or behaviours that could be regarded as 'ceremony' (starting with a handshake)

2. Aside from the Bandywallop case, can you think of any stories or 'symbolic narratives' that people seem to hold precious?

PART II

ELEMENTS

What is 'Evolving Christianity'?

"The Lord went in front of them in a pillar of cloud
by day, to lead them along the way, and in a pillar
of fire by night, to give them light, so that they
might travel by day and by night." (Exod 13:21)

Chapter 4 concluded with our introducing the term 'evolving'. What does this mean? Is it a good term?

We seem to be stuck with the term '*Progressive* Christianity'; I would sooner we were not! However, it is now so widely used that my reservations probably count for little. I am uneasy with terms that seem to have a ring (or even a faint tinkle) of smugness or superiority. After all, no flawed human beings have the right to claim a monopoly on revealed truth. Hence, I would prefer other ways of naming what this trend is all about – because it is a 'trend', a stream of thinking rather than an easily recognisable movement or system. So, what is it about? The short answer is to say that it's about pushing the limits of traditional orthodoxy; indeed, leaping over them. It's a handy term if one is roaming outside what some regard as the boundaries.

As I understand it, Evolving Christianity can be said to rest in the first place on three 'negatory' propositions. First of these is that there is *no question 'off limits'*. When congregations have pursued adult series like 'Living the Questions', participants have felt (often for the first time) that they now had permission to question matters that were previously thought 'taboo'. Not just the virgin birth or the resuscitated corpse, but whether there were women disciples, whether Jesus could have been married, whether God could speak through other faiths, whether there is a God at all!

Second, Evolving Christianity says that there can be *no literature, institution or professional caste above criticism*. This is what the renowned theologian Paul Tillich called 'the protestant principle' – which meant refusal to accept any relative authority as absolute. Tillich said that every church – including those of the 'Reformation', had violated this principle by attributing absoluteness to that which did not deserve it. He referred scathingly to 'the church of the absolutism of the dogma'.

Third, Evolving Christianity says there is *no formulation of the faith that can be considered definitive*. That is to say, there is no 'standard' Christianity by which all that differ from it can or should be judged as heresy, or as deviation from the one true faith. There never will be some single impermeable standard whose supporters can claim to be custodians of the correct faith. What we have are many Christianities which bear more or fewer family resemblances with one another – but the concept of one 'correct' version is repudiated in Evolving Christianity.

So much for the three negatory foundations. What, then, are some of the major areas where no questions are off limits, where no authorities are absolute and where no orthodoxy can be claimed?

The first of these has to do with what we think we mean by 'G-O-D' – especially in the light of modern cosmology. Do the Hebrew and Christian scriptures, and the theological traditions of two thousand years, contain the last word on God? Plainly, the answer is a resounding 'no'. How does 'G-O-D' relate to the cosmos? For instance, did 'G-O-D' (whoever that might be!) wind it up 15 billion years ago and then take an extended holiday? In what sense can we say that 'G-O-D' interacts with the cosmos? What price so-called 'miracles'? Questions about prayer arise here also. What *is* prayer? 'Spirituality' is a big issue in Evolving Christianity.

Second, it has become allowable to ask questions about who Jesus may have thought he was – perhaps in contrast with what scripture or church have said on the subject! Even, following Dan Brown's *The Da Vinci Code*, could Jesus have been married? Can we identify clearly the agenda and message of Jesus? Jesus research says, "Yes, indeed we can!" This line of inquiry commonly leads to repudiating any attribution of divinity to Jesus, not to mention theories of atonement; i.e., we are somehow saved by his blood from the eternal barbecue.

Third, it has become allowable – indeed mandatory in Evolving Christianity to take seriously the existence of other faiths, and to ask questions about the place that other faiths which were once called 'heathen' may have in the divine chemistry. Many Christians are much less confident today about claiming a monopoly on the truths of God. Do faiths like Buddhism, Hinduism, Islam, Judaism and Sikhism have their own integrity as windows to eternal truth? Is it just possible that God may be far more 'versatile' than we have given God credit for being? Could it be possible that we might just learn something from the holy people of other faiths?

For many who have spent a lifetime in churches it has been liberating to be told that these questions are not off limits. Indeed, these same men and women are now the major consumers of works by Spong *et al*, and by Australian writers like Morwood, Webb and Parkinson. My own book *No Fixed Address* could be included here.

The one thing that is unlikely to be extracted from Evolving Christians is any kind of 'creed' – for this would be to violate the third principle above; viz., that there is no formulation of the faith that can be considered 'definitive'. In fact, among those who are happy to gather under the broad canopy of 'evolving' there are many different views on many different aspects of the faith.

At the same time, there is probably a broad consensus on most if not all of the following six 'propositions'. I should think that most 'evolvings' would probably be happy to say that

1. The formula 'G-O-D' denotes something that is eminently real, but defying definition. One can speak of God only in metaphor – and no metaphor must be allowed to become a 'golden calf'.
2. What is said about 'G-O-D' should be logically defensible and consistent with what modern cosmology shows us about the history and nature of the universe.
3. Jesus of Nazareth is a quintessentially God-informed person, in whose life and teaching are keys to the best possible world,

and who does not need to be turned into a god.

4. The Hebrew and Christian scriptures (Old and New Testaments) are testimony to the human quest for ultimate meaning, while at the same time bearing all the marks of human fallibility.

5. The 'church' is that community of people who seek to follow Jesus in deed and word, and to keep alive the rumour of God.

6. The life of faith is a never-ending journey of discovery.

I for one would see the above mentioned as the irreducible *minima* of affirmations if one is to identify with 'Evolving Christianity'. I find it hard to see how anyone can make the claim to be in this stream of thinking while dismissing God, Jesus or scripture – not to mention all three. I realise also that the six axioms listed above may be quite inadequate for some. I stress that they are not intended to be regarded as either exclusive or exhaustive; only as sufficient *for me*!

As part of my own personal 'journey' I laid out 'One Man's Credo', which appeared in *No Fixed Address* (pp.242-3). I include it here not as a manifesto that must be embraced by my reader, but as helping to explain where I am coming from in the present exercise; as being completely open with my reader. What is contained herein determines the shape of *my* teaching and of *my* personal 'spirituality'. It is the 'myth' or sacred story that informs *my* life, and which could help to shape worship for any who decided to claim it as theirs also. However, I must emphasise that it is entitled '*One* Man's Credo'. It is not a test of your faith!

ONE MAN'S CREDO

I believe that
- the self-creating universe conceived in the mind of the cosmos
- burst into being from an unimaginably small point, in unimaginable heat and energy,
- with every possibility and option for its behaviour and

development present in that first micro-millisecond,
• like an embryo at fertilization.

I believe that
• the initial conditions look to have been subtly 'skewed'
• to maximise the likelihood of some possibilities and not others,
• as for a woman with baby in utero,
• on planet earth yielding not merely life, but humanity –
• able to discern and do evil or good, so shaping the future of earth.

I believe that
• this is no accident, but bespeaks divine intention and influence, as in birth and nurture of progeny;
• it should not then surprise when Rabbi Jesus uses the metaphor of cosmic parent,
• or that his followers call him 'son' – as one who bears a filial resemblance,
• and who has rare insight into *the mind of the cosmos* –
• with which his own thought and life are in harmony.

I believe that
• to be religious as Jesus was, and to be an 'authentic' human being, are essentially the same –
• since both come from letting one's mind be conformed to the cosmic mind (Romans 12)
• who continues to help this self-creating universe realise its highest potential
• and move toward an ultimate symphony of creation.

I believe that
• the foregoing points me toward a recovered spirituality,
• resting on the conviction that God may be heard when one listens,
• that in silence one may 'tune' to the cosmic mind,
• complemented by reflecting on tradition, and by admonition and correction with fellow-seekers.

Source: *No Fixed Address: Faith as Journey* (Spectrum 2010) pp.242-3

This is my prayer …

You are the One
in whom the universe was conceived,
who brought it into being,
who set the laws of its behaviour
and who has guided its evolving life.
Help us tune our minds to you
and so find the way
to richer possibilities for ourselves
and for the world in which we dwell.

There are, of course, several implications in 'One Man's Credo' – if I should be on trial down the track for heterodoxy or heresy! In the first place, I am unashamedly a 'theist', and I object strongly to the diminishing of that word by those who equate it with primitive belief in a supernatural entity floating around somewhere out there in the ether; something that looks like a ginormous hot air balloon with **GOD** painted on it! In my glossary of terms there are four major options. You have to be one of these, or maybe an amalgam of two!

- A *theist* believes that the word 'G-O-D' refers to something that is eminently real – although very probably quite beyond definition!
- An *atheist* believes that 'G-O-D' has no counterpart in reality. It is a nonsense word like *qwertyuiop* (top line of a keyboard)
- An *agnostic* believes that there is insufficient evidence to permit a judgement one way or the other about the 'G-O-D' issue.
- An *adiaphorist* believes the whole subject is so silly that it really doesn't deserve a second thought. (look up that word if you don't know it)

In this sense I am a 'theist', and unapologetically so! However, I believe one can speak of the divine only in metaphors, and the metaphor I am inclined to use is 'mind of the cosmos', 'cosmic mind' or (in Greek) *dianoia kosmou*, which is not strictly biblical but is inferred from the conversation between godtalk and cosmology.

That is to say, 'G-O-D' is for me the One who *imagined* a cosmos before it ever was, who *intended* that it should be, who *initiated* it, who *informs* it and who keeps it in being, who *influences* and persuades. I see creation not as an event but as a process (albeit initiated in the so-called 'big bang') which helps explain what the priest-physicist John Polkinghorne refers to as ragged edges. I recall a distinguished rabbi once saying "God never did get it all finished, final, perfect and complete and then back off; we are still somewhere around Friday afternoon in the whole process (i.e. before the sabbath when God took a rest)."

Where Jesus is concerned, I find those classic doctrines like divinity, trinity, atonement – indeed sin, redemption and salvation, unhelpful when they are related to Jesus, but I am at ease with a term Lorraine Parkinson employs; viz., 'god-soaked human being'. It may be remembered that Marcus Borg says we live in God as fish live in the sea. It is important to remember that the sea is in the fish also! I see Jesus' formula for 'the best possible world', as exquisitely laid out in the Sermon on the Mount, to be worthy of whole-hearted embrace as the original gospel of the kingdom! That is to say, Evolving Christianity as I understand it is about the religion *of* Jesus; not the religion *about* Jesus!

And finally, it is here that I feel a great affinity with the Society of Friends (Quakers) – insofar as silence seems to me much more likely to afford access to the holy whispers than the barrage of noise that is characteristic of modern life and indeed of much so-called 'worship'!

In Chapter 6 I say more about Silence. But this is enough for the moment on the sacred story (or 'myth') as I see it. How then might we find suitable ceremony (or 'ritual') to celebrate this? That is the question.

QUESTIONS FOR THOUGHT AND TALK

1. Are you ill at ease with any of the 'negatory' propositions with which this chapter begins?

2. How much (or little) of 'One Man's Credo' are you able to make your own – albeit in different words, if you prefer?

6

Silence

"The Lord was not in the wind ... the earthquake ...
the fire ... but after the fire a sound of sheer silence.
When Elijah heard it, he wrapped his face in his
mantle and went out and stood at the entrance of
the cave. Then there came a voice to him ... "
(I Kings 19:11-13)

Chapter 5 outlined an understanding of what is meant by 'Evolving Christianity' (more often called 'progressive') and the framework of belief that one may like to find in Christian worship. But we have still not answered the vexed question "How shall we do it?" And so this chapter deals with what may seem a rather unusual place to be starting; that is, with the place of *Silence*.

Why in heaven's name (yes, in heaven's name!) do we have to make so much continuous noise in a service of worship? Why this endless exhorting and pronouncing, singing and praying. The lost element in our daily life – and generally in our liturgy is silence, and I submit that we are much the poorer for this. Some of my grandchildren's generation seldom have a plug out of one ear, connected as they are to a constant input of noise. Some claim that they cannot study without this noise, so accustomed have they become to it. They have lost the ability to enjoy silence and to benefit from it. Indeed I wonder if some are not afraid of silence!

In 2005 the BBC screened a TV series that duly came to Australia. Called 'The Monastery', it showed five men on a six-week experience of Catholic monastic life. They lived with 22 Benedictine monks at Worth Abbey in West Sussex. Four of the men ranged from 29-37 in age and one was 69. What they found the toughest aspect of monastic life was the silence. Abbot Christopher Jamison, who directed their 'retreat', reminds us in *Finding Sanctuary* that in the monastic tradition there is a basic background of silence.

> *"where people today commonly have background music, monks have background silence." (p.36)*

Jamison says that the men found being truly silent was not easy to achieve, and that they never really came to grips with it. However, there was a major breakthrough at one point. Their first instinct had been to fill the silence with something; conversation or music were the common ways of drowning out the silence. But after ten days they began to see that silence was offering them something they needed.

> *"So in a moment of drama combined with comedy, they spontaneously handed over their mobile phones and their Walkmans!" (p.37)*

The full account of their experience at Worth Abbey is readily available via the internet, and is not necessary here. Suffice it to say that for all five men there were significant life changes; for at least three of them there were quite massive changes.

In my own case, growing up in the 1930s and 40s without a mobile, a walkman (these days an iPod) or a TV, I have never needed to be persuaded how good silence can be. At the age of nineteen, I was to become even more convinced of this. As I mentioned, my coming into faith at that age was via a house group that practiced the discipline of the 'Quiet Time'. Later I was to introduce hundreds of young people to this at camps and conferences; some who learned the habit fifty years ago have maintained it. These days I belong to a network of meditators, and guard the times of intentional solitude and silence, including my early morning walk.

When I studied in Boston during the 1960s I became familiar with the work of the renowned Bostonian Ralph Waldo Emerson (1803-1882). Emerson was in some respects an 'evolving or progressive christian' before these terms were abroad. Initially a Unitarian minister, he became widely read and heard as writer and lecturer. He was the key figure in the Transcendentalist Club, consisting of bright and articulate younger ministers who criticised traditional religion, protesting against its formalism and dogmatism.

Emerson repudiated the God of authority and of tradition, developing his concept of 'self-reliance'. What this meant to him was not dismissing God, but listening for and heeding the still, small voice within – what I have called 'the holy whispers'. He said, "Let us be silent, that we may hear the whispers of the gods." Hence my inclusion of Emerson in addressing this lost element in our daily life and in our liturgy. The writings of Emerson affected me in more ways than one.

So much for daily life, though; now to liturgy. Where is the silence? I belong to a tradition that appears to believe not only in the power of the Word, but in the power of *words*! If judging by a sample service or two, we could well conclude that 'verbal immersion' was thought to be highly beneficial; the more words, the better. It is rare indeed for a time of formal worship to include elements of quiet, unless these are snippets of 5 to 10 seconds when we reflect on our sins or when we visualise those for whom we are praying. When silences in the liturgy exceed this limit, one can sense the awkwardness. It seems that we do not know what to do with silence.

Perhaps we fear not that the still small voice will be withheld from us, but that it may indeed *be* heard as a holy whisper within – and that could be disturbing! On the other hand, periods of silence present no problems at all to some people of faith. For example, the Taizé monastic community in France, which annually draws thousands of young people, includes substantial periods of silence in its liturgical life, and the Quakers (or Friends) are accustomed to a way of worship where the silence is broken only if a member of the company feels very strongly that he/she has something that merits sharing. I have been at Quaker meetings where nobody spoke.

It should scarcely be necessary to mount a series of arguments for silence; for those who are already convinced, the case is indisputable. Allow me, however, to suggest three reasons for building more silent spaces into our own lives and into our worship.

First is that silence can be *deeply restful and therefore refreshing*. It is not the same as sleep, but in some respects can bring similar benefits. The founder of Pennsylvania was the English Quaker William Penn, who said, "True silence is the rest of the mind, and is to the spirit what sleep is to the body, nourishment and refreshment." When one moves into this kind of silence, body rhythms can slow down; breathing slows and heart rate drops.

In 1689 Penn established in Philadelphia the "William Penn Charter School', one of the oldest and grandest private schools in the US. The students engage regularly in Quaker worship, or what they call 'Meeting'. Emily, who graduated in 2006, describes what this meant for her, both at school and in her local Quaker meeting.

> *"I am a birthright Quaker and attend Meeting outside of school. The purpose of meeting is simple, to slow down. In this day and age especially the amount of 'hustle and bustle' is enormous. Meeting is a time when one can slow down, relax, and contemplate. As I sit in [the school's] meeting, oftentimes I close my eyes and let my brain relax. I wouldn't say I sleep, because it is not the same as 'deep sleep' I achieve at night, but I slip into a semi-concience [sic] form of rest, a kind of mental nirvana. I find it to be very relaxing and also in some cases necessary to calm down my over excited brain."*

It may well be that the best way to begin a liturgical event is in a period of silence for 'healing' – letting go the hurts experienced and putting down the burden of hurts caused – by accident or by intent. In the section on Prayer, where I refer to those things that make us feel 'bad', this is dealt with. It seems to be a fairly obvious place in any liturgical event for a healthy dose of silence!

Somewhat related to the foregoing, but not identical, is a second argument for silence; it provides *a time to clear the head* of all the noise between our ears. In a short prayer I have sometimes used in the early part of a service, which can be said by the leader either before or following a time of silence, the words are

> *"(God), We have careered in here with much clutter and clamour and commotion crowding our heads, and wanting to clear it away that we might hear the whispers of your spirit. We believe you are speaking*

softly and so we will try to listen attentively – in the way of Jesus. This is our prayer. Amen."

A third argument here for silence is foreshadowed in that prayer. It is that we have gathered in the hope of *tuning in to the 'holy whispers'*. Hence Ralph Waldo Emerson's "Let us be silent, that we may hear the whispers of the gods."

There is another kind of silence, which is for the intense concentration of all our energies of heart and soul and mind on those for whom we are called to prayers of care; I shall defer attention to this kind of silence until the chapters on prayer. Meanwhile, I hope the case is clear: that a liturgical event, as with our individual lives, in which there is a torrent of noise to the exclusion of silence is likely to leave us the poorer.

As I indicated earlier, my day begins with a half-hour of silence, when I walk my set route, eyes fixed on the ground before me. Because this is now a familiar and set behaviour, I find in the first 2-3 minutes my head normally emptying of all conscious thought. It is a rather pleasant surprise to realise that one is not thinking – except that once one is thinking 'now I'm not thinking', he **is** thinking! The second stage, while attempting to keep all the normal distractions from entering my head, is when I am purposely attending to 'the holy whispers'.

QUESTIONS FOR THOUGHT AND TALK

1. What do you think has happened in western society over your lifetime for this addiction to noise to have developed?

2. Do you think it is practicable to include periods of silence in Evolving Christian worship? What would be their purpose? What guidance if any would need to be given the worshippers?

7

Doing without Words?

*"When you are praying, do not heap up empty
phrases as the Gentiles do; they think that they will
be heard because of their many words!"
(Matthew 6:7)*

You will by now have guessed that I often find the proprietary lines
of packaged piety, as marketed by churches, somewhat unappealing.
For me and others like me, they tend to obscure rather than reveal
the holy … the sacred … the ineffable mystery around us and within.
I find my sense of this unmeasurable infinity is contracted, distorted,
disfigured by the banal linguistics of so much organised religion.
There, I have said it – and I cannot retract it!

My own memorable 'epiphanies', or revelations, have tended to be
outside churches; not inside them. Let me tell you of one in which
words would have been not only superfluous but bordering obscene.
Early one February morning in 2004 I stopped transfixed at the foot
of my back steps. To the right of me, and about one metre above the
ground, was a gum leaf. It was about 10cm long and little more than
1cm across at its widest part. It was in mid air, apparently weightless,
with no means of support.

But it was not still. It was describing in mid air all the most
stunning of ballet movements. For just a second or two poised *'en
pointe'* as they say in ballet (on the toe). Then pivoting faster and faster
– until it stopped as quickly as it began. Taking giant leaps this way
and that, and then pausing as if to think 'What shall I do next?'

Of course, it was not without means of support. It was suspended on the finest gossamer spun during the night by a spider now gone. The thread was invisible, but I knew it had to be there.

No scientific instruments could have predicted the sequence of movements described in the air by my dancing leaf. Catching the softest breeze, it lifted and spun and leapt and flew with a freedom not even God could have known in advance! For, as with everything else in this universe, its future was 'open'. It had the freedom to be itself. That was my 'dancing leaf' epiphany, and it was a moment of rich early morning worship – without words! Indeed, I have now gone close to destroying the mystique of that moment by the very exercise of setting it down in words. But if that is not easily reducible to words, consider putting any or all of the following into words:

- The taste of ripe strawberries
- The feel of a baby's skin against your own
- The scent of 'Fragrant Cloud' roses pervading the space about them
- The stand of mountain ash soaring upward 100m around you

All these are daily phenomena, readily accessible to experience, but susceptible to verbal description? Of course, not! There is no way one can put these into words; they defy our best efforts, which can only ever be lame and lumbering. And yet, can you believe it, we try to put into words that ineffable reality we dare to name 'G-O-D', as though we can somehow describe this mystery and our sense of it around us and within.

So, what do we manage to produce? We pile words upon words, cliches upon cliches, and end up with a mullock heap of dross from which the gold has long gone. I find myself not only frustrated by much that we call 'liturgy' or 'worship', but worse. I am revolted by its crudeness, its clumsiness, its pretentiousness, its preciousness – to the point where I want to shed it all – and find ways of **wordless** worship, or near wordless worship.

I suspect the answer may be found in a combination of elements – perhaps with music predominating, but using silences and perhaps visual images. To do what? ***To make me aware again of the goodness in myself, the goodness in those around me, the goodness in the world at large that can be harnessed to help achieve the best possible***

outcomes. If worship has any good purpose at all, then surely this is what it is about. But is this possible without a torrent of words? I like to think so. Now to a second 'epiphany', this time in a church, although not in a structured time of corporate worship.

During the infamous presidency of Ferdinand Marcos I was in the Philippines. While in Manila I went in search of the church of St Joseph in Las Piñas City, which was built two centuries ago by an indefatigable Augustinian monk, Father Diego Cera de la Virgen del Carmen. In addition to being a charismatic leader of his people, Father Cera was a multi-skilled man: naturalist, chemist and architect as well as builder.

But he was even more: he was an organist and organ builder. That was the real reason I sat alone in this place one afternoon – listening to the sounds drawn from Father Cera's biggest project: a pipe organ built of bamboo. It took this good man eight years to fashion an instrument unlike any other of its kind – producing wind sounds of exquisite purity from the native flora of his adopted country. Many have said it is one of the finest old organs in the world; Australian organist Douglas Lawrence has been recorded playing it. For an hour in this 'Garden of Eden' I heard the singing bamboo pipes of St Joseph's. Words would have been superfluous; indeed, obscene as in that experience with my dancing leaf.

The two episodes I have recounted – a dancing leaf and a singing organ, are not the stuff of every hour in every day. But they are typical of what I call 'times of special awareness', when the Transcendent somehow becomes more real and powerful than at other times. What these episodes have in common is that in neither case were any words employed to explain or interpret what was happening. The experiences delivered their own meanings. If you can allow yourselves the luxury, I imagine it would be possible for you to lay alongside of my stories plenty of your own – bringing home to you that 'wordless worship' is a genuine possibility!

A chapter on wordless worship would be deficient if no reference were made to dance, especially given my 'dancing leaf' epiphany. It has always struck me as rather ironic that we should stand stock-still while singing Sydney Carter's "Lord of the Dance". This is actually classed as a 'carol', which originally meant a communal dance. It presents the story of God's action as a dance led by one who is our friend through every phase of it. We owe the tune to the Shakers, an 18th century community who got their name from the way they jiggled in worship.

We are apt to see all that as a bit odd, but perhaps it should not seem so odd. It is thought that some of the psalms began as carols; that is, communal dances. Psalm 149 says, "Praise him with drums and dancing." Psalm 150 says, "Praise him with drums and dancing; praise him with harps and flutes." II Samuel 6:5 says, "David and all the house of Israel were dancing before the Lord with all their might, with songs and lyres and harps and tambourines and castanets and cymbals."

My first grandson arrived in 1988 and my second (his cousin) came along six months later. When each was little more than a year old, and walking, I watched them wobble towards a big speaker box in the corner of our living room. By then we had a decent sound system, and must have had something playing. On two separate occasions I watched transfixed as these little boys halted a metre or two from the speaker, paused to listen ten to fifteen seconds and then began to move. Each did it, at little more than a year old! With arms up, they wove from side to side, forward and backward to the music – dancing when they were scarcely able to walk. They could not have learned this; it came naturally. What this suggested to me was that we are 'programmed' to dance. Indeed, not to dance is to deny something God has placed within us.

David and all the house of Israel notwithstanding (above), I would be hard pressed to get an entire congregation up and dancing before the Lord with all their might, but what of specialist liturgical dancing? This can be one of the potentially unsettling issues for the straight-laced, as I was to learn when Dean of our theological school. It was my turn, together with a student, to conduct the Friday eucharist, and as was our custom then, to follow the lectionary. The set gospel was that account in John 3 of a conversation between Jesus and the Pharisee Nicodemus about being 'born again'.

Without going into detail here, I simply report that the student and I decided to consult a well known and highly regarded dancer – ballet trained and a teacher of liturgical dance. She choreographed a very beautiful sequence of moves that symbolised dying and coming alive again. As are all dancers, she was a good looking person, and wore full-length but filmy apparel. In a congregation that numbered about eighty, few had seen liturgical dance, or seen it used so expertly. About one-quarter were deeply moved by it. Some were unsettled by the richly sensuous (not sensual) nature of it. Some took an alternative exit route from the chapel. I was aware that in seeking to communicate a profound religious truth, we were using a means of communication that had big problems for some.

There have been other occasions since then when I have witnessed some beautiful liturgical dance, and I know several who are specialists in the area. Dance may have an important place in Evolving Christian worship and I would not want it dismissed simply because of its unfamiliarity.

If liturgical dance is thought inappropriate for wordless worship, one wonders how art also might be considered eloquent in its own right – especially abstract art. This is not the place to explore links between spirituality and art, but the matter cannot be swept under the rug, especially by Evolving Christianity. Princeton's Robert Wuthnow has been pointing the way with two fairly recent works – *Creative Spirituality* (2001) and *All in Sync* (2003). In the latter he says,

> *"My interviews with rank-and-file Americans suggest that many have been prompted to think about spirituality by participating in the arts or being exposed to the arts as consumers."*

Abstract art, not within our purview here, takes us into the "sombre, borderless canvases" of Mark Rothko and others – suggestive of "deep silence and infinite void, yet somehow evoking a sense of presence and mystery".

In Chapter 9 we look more particularly at music as a key element in our times of special awareness.

QUESTIONS FOR THOUGHT AND TALK

1. Can you recall episodes in your own experience where something visual or something auditory spoke to you of the Transcendent, without the need for words to explain or interpret them?

2. Can you see ways in which we may usefully turn to visual images or symbols, and pieces of music in our 'times of awareness and attentiveness', allowing them to deliver their own message to us without words?

3. Could dance have possibilities for Evolving Christian worship – or is it for you too far out altogether? Can you set down reasons for your answer to this question?

8

Bread and Wine

*"On the first day of the week, when we met to break
bread, Paul was holding a discussion with them"
(Acts 20:7)*

The importance given to what is variously called 'holy communion',
'the eucharist', 'the mass' or 'the Lord's supper' varies hugely between
the different traditions, and it calls for very careful consideration in
Evolving Christianity. Some background to the practice is necessary.
How did it originate?

Notions of 'community' are not exclusive to *homo sapiens*. Animal
species display features of living in community. However, sharing
scarce resources – such as food – is a feature of more highly refined
'communal' behaviour. But it would seem that among even the most
primitive of human beings, eating together is a powerful expression
of such communalism.

Certainly this has a strong history in the culture and faith of Jesus.
Judaism has a tradition of many festivals and celebrations, all of which
are accompanied by eating and drinking together. The most riotous
of all is probably Purim; Rabbi Harold Kushner says there is virtually
an obligation to get drunk at Purim!

And so, eating and drinking together would seem to have been
the commonest expression of communalism for the followers of Jesus.
It is probable that much of his instruction was done in the context
of meals – either with his disciples or in the homes of people who
gave them hospitality. Whatever Jesus did on the occasion that
Christians see as the start of the "Lord's Supper", it would have been

something that was done often and without much formality.

It is thought that the particular occasion alluded to in scripture was probably a Passover meal. The description of it is stylised to fit with the tradition that was already developing, to make the point that a certain bunch of exclusively male followers (!) constituted the core of the movement, and to fit into the 'plot' that unfolds in the gospels. It is very unlikely to have taken place as recounted, either by Paul or by the evangelists. (See extended note at the end of this chapter)

It is also highly unlikely – indeed, impossible in my judgement that Jesus could have intoned words about his body and his blood. Judaism had *no* place for human sacrifice; quite the contrary! This was a pagan rite. The form of the sacrament, whatever we call it, would have been repugnant to Jesus in the style commonly met today. Remember, Jesus was an observant Jew; the Jewish scholar Pinchas Lapide has called him 'the orthodox Jew *par excellence*'!

The history of the sacrament and the diverse forms it now takes can be followed (if anyone is interested) in books on sacramental theology and liturgy. What matters here is that most churches have it in one form or another, and celebrate it with greater or lesser frequency. Churches or 'traditions' which do not have sacraments are the Society of Friends (Quakers) and the Salvation Army.

In the so-called 'reformed protestant' churches, the sacrament generally does not have the somewhat exalted place it has in Anglican, Catholic, Lutheran and Orthodox traditions. Historically, preaching has been given more importance in the protestant traditions and relatively less in the others. In fact, some reformed protestants would have said in times past that preaching was a 'sacrament'; that is, a means of grace!

However, there has been a trend, fostered through the modern ecumenical movement, to give to 'the eucharist', as it is now commonly termed, more importance and also to celebrate it more often. Furthermore, there has been a trend toward adopting a style (words &c) more like that followed in the other traditions. Some reformed protestants have felt comfortable with these developments and others have not; in fact, they have felt very uncomfortable, I being one! One reason for the discomfiture some feel is that the form being advocated implies a set of dogmas about the person and work of Jesus ('Jesus the Christ') which they find problematic. To be explicit, they find it very difficult to affirm these two propositions:

- That Jesus the Christ was 'divine' or the incarnate second person of the blessed trinity – or that he could ever have thought of himself in such terms;
- That his death (and resurrection) somehow in themselves constitute a means of 'atonement' for people otherwise ineligible for fellowship with God.

On the contrary, an increasing number of people like this would much prefer to affirm

- That Jesus, in the words of the late Professor Arthur Peacocke (2001 Templeton Prize winner), is 'the God-informed person *par excellence*.'
- That his exemplifying and teaching a 'love ethic' strikes an answering chord in us, and inspires us to want to be like him.

The first two propositions can be called christology, and the second two cannot be called christology. It is christology that is packaged in the common style of the eucharist, and this is where it is problematic for those who identify with Evolving Christianity.

Many would probably like to find a way to preserve the ritual meal as a celebration of community, and pre-eminently as a celebration of corporate memory. They suspect this may be closer to the heart of Jesus anyway! That is to say, that the emphasis should be everywhere and always upon GOD and listening for God – consistent with what we know of the spirituality of Jesus.

The modern ecumenical movement has expended a great deal of energy on trying to establish common ground with beliefs about sacraments, ordination and so on. Before we go to war (so to speak) over such matters as the ritual meal, it is salutary to consider what was said fifty years ago by the distinguished Quaker and religious educator Harold Loukes.

> *"Most of the negotiations now in train are concerned with matters that do not seem to affect Friends at all: a minimum creed, the status of the priesthood, inter-communion. But this does not mean that Quakers have*

nothing to say while discussions go on. Their task is to lay special emphasis on what has always been true Christian doctrine: that the 'means of grace' are means and not ends: that creeds and priests and mass are channels of spiritual insight, and not in themselves the eternal verities."

I conclude this chapter with what would seem to me to be the irreducible minimum of appropriate words for a eucharist in evolving Christianity. After a word on inclusiveness (not obligatory) there would follow a brief word of explanation and a word of invitation; then a short prayer followed by distribution and sharing of the elements with *no* further word apart from a closing prayer. Following is the way this might proceed.

ON INCLUSIVENESS

(a background note that may or may not be used)

It seems that Jesus ate with all, setting aside social distinctions. He left a tradition of inclusiveness and equality in the Kingdom, marked by a new kind of meal arrangement. He spoke of the coming age as a banquet for all. Among early followers there was a custom of communal eating, without ritual connection to Passover or his death. ★ *I invite you to see the sharing of bread and wine in this way.*

WORD OF EXPLANATION

From the earliest human life, sharing food and drink has meant survival and gratitude, community and loyalty – nutriment for body and for spirit. For Jesus and his companions, bread and wine from earth spoke of the Creator. It spoke of their forbears' escape from slavery and long march in the wilderness. It bonded them in a common commitment to listen for the Voice. After Jesus' death, it was a time to remember him, to recall their common purpose, to be renewed.

WORD OF INVITATION

The meaning of the meal together has not changed. Let the bread and wine be as provisions for a journey, a reminder of the Mystery around us and within, an echo of the Voice that says, "I have called you." This bread and wine is for all who would listen to that voice.

PRAYER

We are thankful for every meal that has replenished us in body and spirit. We are thankful for the life and teaching of Jesus, who has brought us to this table. We are thankful for these elements, which carry a holy and a healing word for each of us. As we receive them, may our faith and hope and love be reinvigorated. This is our prayer. **AMEN**

Bread and wine served with no more words, but after partaking all say …

PRAYER

Eternal One, who gives us bread and wine, may we hear you in the day-by-day, and there respond – that the world for which you hope may come. This is our prayer. **AMEN**

★ *According to The Didache, an ancient Christian document*

QUESTIONS FOR THOUGHT AND TALK

1. Do you think that in some form the ritual meal with bread and wine is an essential aspect of all or most liturgical events? If not all, but some, what might these be?

2. If you were trying to craft some suitable words to go with the sharing of bread and wine, how would you put this? Would it be possible to have a 'eucharist' with exceedingly few words?

NOTE ON THE 'INSTITUTION' OF THE LORD'S SUPPER

The 'synoptic' gospels all have an account of the 'institution' of the ritual meal (Matthew 26:26-30, Mark 14:22-26, Luke 22:14-20). John has a long discourse taking place in the context of a final meal, but no 'words of institution'. These seem to be drawn from Paul in I Corinthians 11:23-26.

I have grave doubt that this material comes from Paul. We have no original Pauline letters, but only copies of copies of copies – and we know how copyists made the occasional editorial changes! For instance, the trinitarian baptismal formula in Matthew 28 is obviously a late addition; Jesus would never have said anything remotely like this.

My own view is that Jesus and the disciple band (including wives and other women, and possibly children) would often have eaten together, and would have had prayers with the meal – as is the case today at a Jewish meal table. But the words of 'institution' with which we seem to be stuck today are probably not from Paul, definitely not from Jesus and should be set aside in Evolving Christianity.

9

MUSIC

"Be filled with the Spirit, as you sing psalms and hymns and spiritual songs among yourselves, singing and making melody to the Lord in your hearts." (Eph.5:18b-19)

'Would Jesus have sung?' is like asking 'Is the Pope a Catholic?' The longest book in the Bible is a collection of Hebrew songs (Psalms), leaving us in no doubt that music was intrinsic to the religion of Jesus. The psalms were his 'hymn book', which is one reason I like their continued use in some form or another. Matthew's account of the last supper ends with "when they had sung the hymn, they went out to the Mount of Olives."

In fact, music is mentioned in the Hebrew and Christian scriptures over 800 times. In the former David is portrayed as bard, musician and dancer (II Samuel 6:14); tradition has it that he authored many of the psalms. Miriam the prophet was also a skilled musician – who led the women of Israel in song and dance. Solomon is said to have written over 1000 songs and to have employed 120 priest-trumpeters.

Music seems to have been a feature of innumerable social gatherings, both informal and formal. For instance,

- Departing guests could be sent on their way 'with mirth and songs, with tambourine and lyre.' (Gen.31:27)
- The prosperous enjoyed their leisure 'singing with tambourine and lyre, and rejoicing to the sound of the pipe.' (Job 21:12)
- It was common among banqueting guests 'to sing songs to

the sound of the harp, and like David to improvise on instruments of music.' (Amos 6:5)

- It was a feature of funerals. 'Send for the skilled women to come; let them quickly raise a dirge over us.' (Jer 9:17-18)
- Music was also a feature of coronations. 'All the people went up following him [Solomon] playing on pipes and rejoicing with great joy.' (I Kings 1:40)

It was its introduction to temple worship that gave music its greatest importance for the Jewish people and promoted its development. According to the Hebrew scriptures it was David who first established and regulated the temple music. When the Ark of the Covenant was lodged in Jerusalem, he ordered the Levites to choose from among their number singers who were also instrumentalists. (I Chronicles 15:16-24) In I Chronicles 23:5 we are told that 4,000 Levites were selected to praise God with instruments. Even allowing for exaggeration, temple music was grand and hearty in anyone's terms!

We know little about the actual nature of this early Hebrew music. What does seem to be clear is that singing would have been in unison. Harmony and counter-point were unknown. Variety came partly by means of antiphonal singing (e.g., Psalms 13, 20, 38, 68, 89), but also from the different sounds yielded by instruments. These were of three types: stringed, wind and percussion. Of the first, the *kinnor* was a favourite; the historian Josephus says this was a ten-stringed instrument on which a plectrum was used. The *nebel* had twelve strings and was played by fingers, more like a harp. The commonest wind instrument was the *chalil*, a pipe blown on festal and solemn occasions, and also in mourning. It may have been a simple flute, with holes along it, or could have been a reed instrument more like our oboe and clarinet.

It is probable that the music was loud and strident. Synagogue choirs today generally sing more vigorously than church choirs! The Hebrew word in the psalms that we translate "make a joyful noise" *(rua)* more correctly means to shout at the top of one's voice! The music was probably strongly rhythmical also, if we are to judge from the plethora of drums, triangles, castanets, sistra and cymbals mentioned in the scriptures. Following Manfred Clynes in (Chap 3), it is likely that these percussive rhythms and fairly simple melodies would have generated strong emotional responses in keeping with the passion of the people's literature. One thinks of the crypto-rock music found today in pentecostal and evangelical churches!

This is the background to a tradition of music in Christian worship. We sing because Jesus and his colleagues sang. We have music because this was intrinsic to the religion of Jesus. So it is that Yale historian Jaroslav Pelikan says,

> *"Of all the arts, the one that has had the most continuous positive relation with Christian faith and theology is music."*
> (Jaroslav Pelikan, The Melody of Theology: A Philosophical Dictionary. Cambridge, Mass.: Harvard Univ. Press, 1988, 165)

Specifically Christian music cannot be said to have originated at a particular time and place, since its development has been partly a matter of evolution, but its major antecedent obviously is the tradition in which Jesus belonged. The early Christians used some of the Old Testament canticles; e.g., The Song of Moses in Exodus 15:1-19. ('canticle', from the Latin *canticum* or 'song' is a hymn taken from scripture). Among the best known of New Testament canticles, still preserved in Catholic and Anglican traditions, are the Benedictus (Luke 1:68-79), the Magnificat (Luke 1:46-55) and the Nunc Dimittis (Luke 2:29-32).

During the Middle Ages a rich hymnody developed, known as 'Gregorian chant', after the Pope at the time. Western churches introduced four-part harmony and then with the Reformation there came a wealth of new hymns from such as Isaac Watts and Charles Wesley. Meanwhile in the 17th and 18th centuries some of the world's great composers were producing. Bach's most famous mass was the 'B Minor'. Scarlatti introduced the cantata, a kind of religious musical. Handel created the oratorio, most famously 'The Messiah'. Mozart wrote eighteen masses and Haydn fourteen – his most famous being 'The Creation'. Priest-composers included Allegri, Vivaldi and Soler.

In the 18th century religious music expanded beyond all bounds. Common melodies and even secular or popular songs were borrowed, with religious words being set to them. Black Americans brought 'spirituals' into the range of Christian music, and in the late

20th century there was a veritable epidemic of new church music; ironic given that the Western world was witnessing a decline of interest in organised religion.

A popular form of contemporary music, although lacking the widespread appeal of choruses and crypto-rock one finds in the evangelical and pentecostal churches, comes from the ecumenical monastic community at Taizé in Burgundy (France). These simple refrains are sung over and over, but softly as befits a meditative style of worship, and a selection of them is found in the Australian hymnal *Together in Song*. The content may not be to every taste, but the style merits consideration. For those in search of suitable material there is an appendix on page 122, courtesy my wife Dr Lorraine Parkinson who has listed hymns from four well-known sources that most identified with Evolving Christianity should find acceptable.

Whether it is better to sing oneself, to hear a choir or to listen to a piece of music must be decided by the people concerned. Folk who have impaired bellows and larynx would sometimes sooner not be expected to sing. Folk with uncertain pitch and fragile confidence would sooner not be expected to sing. Folk with too rational and analytical an attention to the words would sooner not be expected to sing – some pieces, any how. I belong to the last mentioned, and quietly decline to sing some hymns!

But all of us are born musical. Our musical tastes begin to form *in utero*. At twelve weeks the auditory system of a foetus is functioning, and it can hear music through the amniotic fluid. I understand that one year olds display clear preferences for music they heard in the womb! When he opened the Centre for Music, Mind and Wellbeing at the University of Melbourne in 2010, Prof Gary McPherson said,

> *"Neurological evidence shows how every normal healthy human is musical, while studies involving the foetus suggest that music might be the first intelligence to reveal itself. There is even speculation that the type of communicative musicality we see between mothers and their newborns provides one of the key moments in our development that subsequently shapes our emotions, and the type of person we eventually become. Some even believe that because music has such a*

*deeply emotional component that it may have evolved before language. Whatever might be true, we know that music-making must have developed for a specific reason and purpose – we just don't know what it is yet."**

Perhaps one reason/purpose is that we can employ it in times of *awareness and attentiveness.* This is where we need the help of our best wordsmiths and musicians with finding new ways we might sing our faith. For those who still prefer to listen, the choice of vocal (solo or choral) and instrumental music calls for sensitivity and skill.

This is where I wish to introduce for consideration my long-held hunches about the flute as a kind of religious 'icon'. It is well known that Aristotle didn't like the flute, but I love it. Aristotle famously observed that "the flute is not an instrument that has a good moral effect. It is too exciting!" With that I must heartily disagree.

Mozart wrote concertos for flute and Bach wrote sonatas for flute. I find some of the most gloriously uplifting music to be that which has been composed for flute. The instrument has an ancient history. Early flutes made of bone have been reliably dated at 37,000 years old, making them probably the oldest known musical instruments – that is made to produce melody, as distinct from some drums and other noise-makers. The flute itself is inert and dumb until the musician blows into it, symbolising for me what we read in the older creation 'myth'.

"The Lord God formed man from the dust of the ground, and breathed into his nostrils the breath of life; and the man became a living being." (Gen.2:7)

Hence my suggestion that the flute can be seen as a type of 'icon'. For me the most haunting flute music, as I indicated in Chapter 2, is produced by the shakuhachi or Zen flute, but any flute or even recorder (often taught to primary school children) can yield the type of sound that I find conducive to awareness and attentiveness. Any Zen flute music played by Grand Master Riley Lee is helpful to meditation, or simply peace of mind; my favourite CD, which has ten tracks is called "Alone … with the Grand Master of CALM."

I want to conclude this section with reflections on music some of which would not be considered strictly 'religious', much less

'Christian' – but which I find profoundly nourishing to the soul, and which I commend for use in collective 'times of awareness and attentiveness'. The following short list is by no means exhaustive, but it is illustrative of the types of music I find evocative of various good 'states' like wonder, gratitude, tranquillity and even aspiration. I list some of my favourite pieces, in no particular order of importance. However, it is probably unsurprising if I begin with Johann Sebastian Bach! Pablo Casals once said,

> *"The miracle of Bach has not appeared in any other art. To strip human nature until its divine attributes are made clear, to inform ordinary activities with spiritual fervour, to give wings of eternity to that which is most ephemeral; to make divine things human and human things divine; such is Bach, the greatest and purest moment in music of all time."*

What follows, with a spot of explanation in each case, is my list of ten pieces that all speak powerfully to me of transcendence. I should add that I also listen with great benefit to Welsh choral hymnody, but will not list details here.

J.S.Bach: Air on a G String *from Orchestral Suite 3 in D major.* This was written by Bach around 1717-23. The late 19th century violinist August Wilhelmj transposed the piece so that he could play it on one string; viz., the G string. Hence its title – and the irresistible 'lesson' that one string can deliver great music. Get it?

J.S.Bach: *10th movement of Cantata No. 147: 'Jesu, Joy of Man's Desiring.'* This is the English title of the cantata *Herz und Mund und Tat und Leben.* The words commonly heard in English are 'Jesu, joy of man's desiring, holy wisdom, love most bright; drawn by thee, our souls aspiring soar to uncreated light'. These are not a translation of the German, but were written by poet laureate Robert Bridges. It matters little, given that the music itself is the source of inspiration.

Gregorio Allegri: *Miserere.* This is a setting of Psalm 51 (Have mercy), familiar for its soaring top C sung by one voice and commonly associated these days with a boy treble. It is a straight acknowledgement of our human frailty and a good alternative to a laboured prayer of confession!

Antonin Dvořák: *Symphony No. 9 in E Minor 'From the New World'.* Dvořák composed this on a visit to the USA during 1892-95, where he was greatly taken by native American music and black spirituals; of the latter he said, "these beautiful and varied themes are the product of the soil. They are the folk songs of America and your composers must turn to them." A theme from the largo is popularly associated with the spiritual 'Goin' Home'.

Ross Edwards: *Dawn Mantras.* Edwards (b.1943) is an Australian who has composed a wide variety of music. Dawn Mantras, also known as Breath of the Spirit, was composed for the dawn performance that took place on the sails of the Sydney Opera House at sunrise on the first day of the new millennium. It conveys a message of hope. It was first performed by shakuhachi, tenor saxophone and didjeridoo, with Sydney Children's Choir and Sydney Chamber Choir, plus child soprano.

G.F.Handel: *Serse (Xerxes): Ombra mai fu.* In this opera the Persian ruler Xerxes sings his ode to a plane tree. Ombra mai fu means 'never was a shade'. Xerxes sings 'shade there never was of any plant dearer and more lovely, or more sweet.' For someone as crazy as I am, who feels an affinity with all things growing, this is a very evocative piece.

Jules Massenet: *Méditation from opera Thaïs.* The monk Athanaël, whose motives are mixed (whose aren't?) ostensibly wishes that Thaïs would convert. Before she follows him into the desert this is played between scenes. The ambiguity of Athanaël's situation is mirrored in the music, which begins sedately and twice has a passionate climax! Maybe a little too much for some congregations, but perhaps they need not know the entire story!

Wolfgang Mozart: *Ave Verum Corpus.* Written in 1791, this is for me the classic example of why it is better not to know the words being sung! A Catholic eucharistic hymn, in translation it says, "Hail, true Body, born of the Virgin Mary, who has truly suffered, and was sacrificed on the cross for mankind, whose side was pierced, whence flowed water and blood, be for us a foretaste of heaven, during our final trial, O Jesu sweet, O Jesu merciful, O Jesu son of Mary, have mercy on me." Better if you don't know Latin!

Camille Saint-Saëns: *Carnival of the Animals, The Swan.* Saint-Saëns would allow only this one piece from Carnival of the Animals to be played while he was alive, arguing that all the rest were too frivolous and could damage his reputation! There is a poignancy in this music which is sometimes thought to express the ephemeral nature of life.

Giuseppe Verdi: *'Va, pensiero, sull'ali dorate' from opera Nabucco (Nebuchadnezzar) Act III.* Sometimes called Chorus of the Hebrew Slaves, it is inspired by Psalm 137, which begins 'By the rivers of Babylon, where we sat down and wept.' Nabucco depicts the Jews' captivity in Babylon after the fall of the first temple in Jerusalem, and this chorus is a moving freedom song of people longing for restoration in the place they loved.

"Wordless Worship" (Chap 7) seems to me to be possible, but worship without music is an oxymoron! For further reading, consult

- Steele, Bruce. *Music & The Church.* Bell Tower Publications (St Aidan's Uniting Church, North Balwyn). 2004
- Steele, Bruce. *Singing The Psalms in The Twenty-first Century.* Bell Tower, 2005

QUESTIONS FOR THOUGHT AND TALK

1. What do you see as the principal reason for singing as an ingredient in 'times of awareness and attentiveness'?

2. Are there particular pieces of music (choral or instrumental) that you find specially conducive to being 'worshipful'?

* *UskoMus is a research network established at the University of Turku, Finland, by the departments of musicology and comparative religion to promote scholarly investigation of relationships between music, religion and spirituality. In December 2010 it sponsored a conference at the Sibelius Museum on "Music and Transcendence".*

10

Scripture

"All scripture is inspired by God and is useful for teaching, for reproof, for correction, and for training in righteousness." (II Tim.3:16)

Alejandro Amenabar's film "Agora", set in 4th century Alexandria, graphically depicts the hostility between defenders of science and reason, and defenders of a faith that has been given imperial legitimacy by Constantine. The central figure is Hypatia, female Alexandrian philosopher and cosmologist/mathematician – a major problem for Christians who take the view that women cannot teach men!

Because Hypatia refuses to convert, Bishop Cyril condemns her. In the film she is stoned to death by church leaders before the altar. This is actually a sanitized version; in fact Hypatia was flayed alive and her remains dragged through the streets! My friend and colleague David Merritt, leader in Evolving Christianity, has this to say of "Agora":

> *"The dominant memories are the horrifying scenes of the Christians destroying the greatest library of the ancient world with its rich store of scientific and philosophical knowledge, and the use of the Bible (in this case the New Testament) as literally the Word of God to forbid an outstanding woman scholar and teacher to teach and then to encourage a 'Christian' mob to butcher her and burn her body parts.*

> *"The idea of the Bible as in any sense Word of God has exacted a terrible price in damaged and destroyed humanity! We should be*

doing more to rid religion of this pernicious sacralising of human
ideas."   (Personal correspondence)

What are we to say about the place of Hebrew and Christian scriptures in Evolving Christianity? Lest anyone say that the Hebrew scriptures do not belong, be it noted that these were the **only** scriptures available to the early Jesus movement. They are, of course, the scriptures to which reference is made in the second letter of Timothy (above). There were no Christian writings at all until I and II Thessalonians in the early 50s, and the earliest gospel (Mark) was written at least twenty years later again. The Hebrew scriptures were Jesus' bible, and to dismiss them should be unthinkable!

However, much of the Hebrew scripture is time and culture specific, and needs to be carefully read in context. In the first place, it was not written for us (neither was the New Testament!), and there are many allusions, notions and prescriptions that do not stand up to scrutiny under the light of Jesus' own teachings.

In *The Sins of Scripture*, John Shelby Spong addresses texts that have often been misused to justify injustice, hatred, mistreatment of the planet, child abuse, sexism, antisemitism and violence! Spong points out that the presence of such texts (even carefully interpreted) raises a fundamental problem with referring to scripture as "God's Word".

My own view is that much of scripture is at best unedifying and at worst potentially toxic – and should therefore be heard **only** if this is to highlight the way religions grow and change! I can see no justification for our having to undergo much of it unless attention is on issues that relate to a proper understanding of scripture, such as questions like the following, which are often asked by earnest seekers!

1. Does the Bible endorse cruel practices?
2. Who actually wrote the Bible?
3. Is the Bible accurately 'translatable' from original languages?
4. Is it appropriate to call the Bible 'God's Word'?
5. Is the Bible 'sexist'?
6. For whom was the Bible written?
7. How does the Bible regard the body?
8. Who decided what should get into the Bible?

9. Are there subjects where the Bible is useless?

10. How should I do my own Bible reading and study?

The Lectionary, to which some preachers are firmly attached, has been touted as a celebration of ecumenism; also as guaranteeing that the faithful will hear much of scripture that would otherwise never be brought to their notice. But why should it be brought to their notice? The intoning of clustered pieces of scripture that are but loosely connected (and sometimes falsely so) is an obscene waste of time. Not only that; it may confirm for many a hearer the impression that scripture has no relevance at all to their lives. Perhaps no one listens, any how! If there are compelling reasons for rigidly following the lectionary, I have yet to hear these.

However, there are purple passages aplenty that can be unpacked over long periods of time for their applicability to the life of faith; for example, one could take all year over the Sermon on the Mount (Matthew 5-7), and start over again with it twelve months later! Some splendid books are available on this; e.g. Lorraine Parkinson's *The World According to Jesus*. When I was chaplain with the University of Melbourne I preached for an entire semester on I Corinthians 13, and for several weeks on just one verse – Philippians 4:8!

> *"Finally, beloved, whatever is true, whatever is honorable, whatever is just, whatever is pure, whatever is pleasing, whatever is commendable, if there is any excellence and if there is anything worthy of praise, think about these things."* (NRSV)

But there is a further option. This is to see the scriptures as a major *resource* to be consulted when people are asking big questions. The syllabus of subjects considered in worship is then driven by the issues exercising them – rather than taking the form of dull commentary on set passages! I would put aside the lectionary, full stop!

A small but not insignificant point is that if scripture is to be read aloud, this needs to be done very well, as befits great literature. As an itinerant pewsitter I regularly hear scripture mercilessly eviscerated by mournful, expressionless lectors, sometimes barely audible and almost invariably exhibiting no sense at all of what the material is about. In consequence the reading of scripture, which modernity seems to dictate should be shared around all and sundry, has become an even more depressing aspect of worship than the preaching!

> *"Have you not known? Have you not heard? The Lord is the everlasting God, the Creator of the ends of the earth. He does not faint or grow weary; his understanding is unsearchable."*

(Isa.40:28)

Have you not known? Have you not heard ... that the scriptures (albeit translated from the original) are replete with high drama, poetry and news headlines? Have you not heard that they contain scorching invective, riveting narratives, lyrical love poetry, hell-fire threats, gentle persuasion, anguished cries of despair, songs of jubilation? Have you not known that they are rich in colourful characterisations – Jacob the cheat, Delilah the temptress, Joseph the upstart, Magdalene Jesus' intimate, Peter the ruffian, Sarah the earth mother? You would not know or hear, for it is rare indeed to be excited by the reading of scripture.

For most of us who have to endure the readings, exceptions stand out memorably. I once attended evensong in the crypt of St. Paul's, London. Pieces were read from Amos 5:21-24 *("I hate, I despise your festivals, and I take no delight in your solemn assemblies")* and from Matthew 25:31-46 *("Just as you did not do it to one of the least of these")* by professional actors! The effect was electrifying. On the way out I said to my late wife, "I'll never read scripture aloud again!" "Yes, you will, but you will do it a whole lot better." I did.

What of other literature – 'religious' or otherwise? There is no doubt in my mind that much illumination and inspiration can be drawn from the sacred literature of other religious traditions – but also from literature we do not normally consider religious. One of my colleagues has said that he finds the so-called 'Canon' of scripture an absurdity – effectively limiting God to addressing us exclusively via this material, and he has quoted in a sermon from the sayings of Confucius!

QUESTIONS FOR THOUGHT AND TALK

1. With what wording would you introduce and conclude readings from scripture in a service of worship? 'This is the Word of God'? (I rather hope not!)

2. Name some pieces of literature not scriptural which in your view are illuminating and inspirational. Could you see them being read in worship?

11

Prayer – Part I

"Do not worry about anything, but in everything by prayer and supplication with thanksgiving let your requests be made known to God." (Philippians 4:6)

Two chapters are given to this subject because it goes to the very heart of what we believe to be our relationship with God.

Most traditional services contain sundry 'prayers' as they are called, ostensibly fashioned to express the assorted nuances of this relationship. The usual are prayers of adoration and/or thanksgiving, plus prayers of confession, petition/supplication and intercession – and also a prayer dedicating the gifts of money. I explain below why most of these terms should be replaced in Evolving Christian worship. In the order for eucharist or holy communion there are more 'prayers', of course. Sometimes there will be another one after the sermon if the preacher thinks of something that he/she has omitted and wants to tack this on!

> **But what exactly do we think we are doing when these prayers are said – either in unison (as with the 'Our Father') or on our behalf by someone presiding?**

Those who know where my journey has led me are aware that I see *listening for the holy whispers* as the heart of prayer. However, it is also important to express ourselves in acts of prayer such as those that form part of a liturgical event. Such prayers commonly find their content in the things that make us feel bad (confession), glad (thankfulness), mad and sad (petition and intercession). It is important to identify and acknowledge these things. But is this because God does not know about them, and must be alerted and informed? Obviously, no! Do we need to *tell* God anything? Hardly!

In my hallway is a mosaic by my daughter Helen. About 25cm square and containing over 1000 coloured 'tesserae' (chips), this depicts the eye of an owl. It replicates part of a work called "Landscape with Birds" by Marcello Provenzale (17th century) in Florence. The eye meets all who enter my house. The 'all-seeing eye' is an ancient metaphor for God. People of faith believe that nothing is hidden from God. In the same way the mosaic could depict an ear, for nothing is unheard by God. If God is God, this must be the case. Whatever we think we mean by 'G-O-D', the notion of a myopic or hearing-impaired divinity is nonsensical. Yet listening to the long and often loud recitals called 'prayer' one could be pardoned for thinking God was blind, deaf and maybe somnolent as well.

The psalmist says "*Hear* me when I call" (Ps.4:1), "The Lord has *heard* my supplication" (Ps.6:9), "The poor man cried and the Lord *heard*" (Ps.34:6). Rather less often does he sing "and you scattered my foes" – although sometimes he longs for that to happen! The psalms are more about getting something off one's chest than they are about getting God to change the course of history or the weather patterns – in response to our pleading or persuading. This is particularly the case with the so-called 'psalms of lament'. *The psalmist believes God is a good listener*!

What of the question 'Does God *answer* prayer?' I 'answer' the door when someone knocks, 'answer' the phone if there is a ring, 'answer' my wife when she calls my name. But what do we mean by this question when it is asked about God and prayer? Is the questioner asking if God complies with specific requests by intervening in the processes of the universe to deliver what is requested? All the evidence would seem to point only one way. The idea of a 'tinkering' God may give comfort to some and even stimulate spiritual practices, but it is an illusion.

Arguments for God 'intervening' in response to pleading or directions from us are based on instances that are more correctly regarded as good luck, coincidence or (in health matters) medical exception. Attributing these to saintly intercession as by Sister Mary

McKillop, and/or to divine intervention, is to imply a God who is whimsical at best and biased at worst; in either case, hardly worthy to be called God. Evolving Christianity repudiates this idea.

For every individual who is favoured with a good experience that seems to have followed on prayer, there are millions equally or more virtuous who have pleaded fruitlessly. My reply to the person who asks "Does God *answer* prayer?" is clearly "No"; that is unless he/she means by *answer* something like my going to the door or to the phone, or acknowledging my wife when she calls my name. But this is not to say that God does not 'hear' prayer. As I have tried to make clear above, I am persuaded that God hears prayer – and this in itself is what makes the practice worthwhile.

At the human level, sharing with another or with others those things that leave us feeling bad, sad or mad (even 'glad' also!) can be very health-giving. We don't expect much of the other apart from *listening* patiently. Now and again we do all the talking, and the other does all the listening! It is actually this which I believe happens when I compose a prayer of confession, a prayer of thankfulness, a prayer of intercession (i.e., for somebody else) or a prayer of petition (i.e., for myself). The very act of prayer can help to discharge toxic emotions, and to tap into good emotions, positive attitudes and springs of energy. All of these can be regarded as God-given, ever-present but sometimes overlooked and missed. Now, another question.

I am often asked the best way to start a prayer. 'To whom do we think we are speaking?' is an entirely reasonable question if we are discussing prayer. It has been customary in my lifetime for spoken prayers, especially in a liturgical event, to begin with some mode of address to God. This was often 'O God, our heavenly father', and was then followed by the content of the prayer. It was like starting a letter 'My Dear Alonso' and then proceeding to tell Alonso what was on my mind. Although 'father' seems to have been for Jesus a favourite metaphor, and although it suits some, not everyone likes it.

Some wish for a mode of address that is gender-neutral – or they even dislike their fathers and consequently it's an uncomfortable metaphor. An alternative in those cases might be 'Eternal God'. When the word 'Lord' is used, this seems often to be ambiguous – variously denoting God or Jesus, depending on the religious style of the one praying.

I have a problem with any and all modes of address for God. I suspect this originates in my addiction to that story of Moses' mystical experience before the burning bush (Exodus 3:1-15). Blazing and crackling furiously, symbol of immense heat and energy (like the big bang?), the bush is not consumed; it is inextinguishable. Moses slinks towards it, but hears a voice. "No further, Moses! You're in a holy place." Moses covers his face. There ensues a conversation between Moses and the Voice, who tells him that he is to lead his people out of enslavement in Egypt. When Moses asks for ID, the Voice says, "I will be who I will be." (*not* 'I am who I am'). This cryptic statement is intended to say "You will never be so familiar with me as to know or use my personal name!"

So, although I say that God is nearer to us than breath itself, that we live in God and God lives in us, to know God's personal name implies a familiarity that none dare claim – even the most spiritual and saintly of any religious tradition. God must forever be the un-nameable one. God must forever be the unutterable mystery. Therefore, insofar as we want to speak of God, or to God, we can only ever use metaphors and metaphorical language, and even then with reservation. If it helps those for whom and with whom we pray, then by all means use a mode of address – but remember that this can only be metaphorical language.

If Moses felt somewhat daunted in this mystical experience, I can be no less so when I believe I am addressing the Eternal! Although I have been ordained fifty-six years, and for longer than that have been composing prayers, I find the exercise at least as challenging as fashioning a sermon. In one I am daring to speak on behalf of God to the listening people – a terribly presumptuous thing to do, but that's preaching. In the other (praying) I am daring to speak on behalf of these people to God. Unless this is just some kind of mechanical intoning of religious phrases (unfortunately, much liturgical prayer is!), I find it as scary as offering a sermon.

So, even though some of my prayers may be couched in fairly

everyday terms, and to be unadorned with the richly poetic splendour of earlier prayer language, I can assure the reader that every word and phrase has been carefully thought through. I shall share here a pet peeve of mine. This is when someone turns to me in a gathering where it is thought appropriate to sanctify the proceedings with an instant prayer. "You will lead us in prayer, John, won't you." That is all the warning I get. I have no opportunity to think it through beforehand, but I am expected to generate a fine flow of pious-sounding phrases off the top of the head, because I am 'in the business' and should be able to do that. If this sounds like a graceless way to speak of those who accord me the privilege of *ex tempore* praying, then so be it; I'm just not comfortable with being unprepared.

How important is it to get the right words at start and conclusion of a prayer – at least in a liturgical event? I had what seemed rather like a conversation with God about the matter recently. That probably sounds silly and pretentious; however, it was in the context of my early morning walk, and it had a certain reality about it that at least some will understand. I hasten to say that I do *not* believe that I have a hot line to heaven, much less that everything entering my head is divinely-authored. So, what happened?

For all I have said above about knowing God's personal name and about 'familiarity' with God, I still have a personal preference for calling God something rather than nothing, and in my quiet prayer sometimes say 'Ground of All Being'. So it was that this exchange took place in my head. "Ground of all Being, is there a mode of address you would prefer?" "No, I have no preference in the matter. It is of small account to me – just so long as you don't think you have somehow 'defined' me by the name you use."

"So, it's OK to call you by whatever seems to describe the way I see our relationship?" "You've got it. People give me all sorts of names. I don't mind what they call me, but I prefer that they don't think they have encapsulated me in that word." "OK, that is reassuring; I know how different people see their relationship with you in different ways."

"You've said it yourself. You know how your progeny call you 'Dad' and your grandchildren call you 'Pop'. Some relatives call you 'John' and others call you 'Uncle John'. Most friends and colleagues call you 'John', and the occasional old school mate calls you 'Bert'. Your wife calls you 'Sweetie'. Then there are those who call you 'Dr Bodycomb'. They all address you in the way that expresses the relationship they have with you – but none of those modes of address (or even all of them put together) define who you are."

As I said, whether or not I heard the Voice that breathed o'er Eden, I've no way of knowing – but it was a good moment, and I share it for that reason. Naturally, the way people think about God is important to me. I don't want any of us to invent a divinity in our own image, or for that matter to bow down before a golden calf (as in worship of dogma) – pitfalls always awaiting us. But for everyone I want an understanding of God that is both worthy of God and expresses a good relationship with God.

So it is that my prayers start in various ways and end in various ways. I no longer wish to argue fiercely for some ways and fiercely against other ways. In passing, what about praying in 'tongues'? Although I do not belong in the pentecostal stream, I want to drop in a word here about praying in tongues. My late friend Krister Stendahl, one time Dean of Harvard Divinity School and Bishop of Stockholm, who died in 2008, said to me, "If some were not so fiercely opposed to glossolalia (tongues) and others were not so fiercely in favour, we might find tongues a much more common feature of spirituality." The value of tongues is not the 'high' that sometimes accompanies this practice, but the fact that this is a language for expressing the inexpressible; as such, it merits consideration.

I've had difficulty all these years also with finding the most appropriate way to conclude prayers. In the fourth gospel we read this statement attributed to Jesus: "I will do whatever you ask *in my name*, so that the Father may be glorified in the Son. If *in my name* you ask me for anything, I will do it." (John 14:13-14). There are lots of references in scripture to doing something 'in the name'; this is a common expression. It is probably what underlies the concluding of Christian prayers with "We ask this in the name of Jesus" or the more grandiloquent piety of "We ask this in the glorious and blessed name of Jesus Christ our precious Lord and Saviour." Perhaps even a few more words than that!

My difficulty with this conclusion to a prayer is that it casts Jesus in the role of intercessor or mediator on our behalf – the One who dies for us and pleads at the throne of grace for us. I do not subscribe to this 'christology' and therefore have a problem with these concluding phrases. Sometimes I feel it could be appropriate to say something like "May our prayer be consistent with the Jesus way", but the intention there is quite different. So, how will the faithful know that one is finished and that it is time to come aboard with 'Amen'? These days I am inclined to say, as does Dr Francis Macnab of St Michael's in Melbourne, 'This is our prayer', to which the response is 'Amen'.

QUESTIONS FOR THOUGHT AND TALK

1. How do you feel about the statement that God hears prayers but does not answer prayers – by some sort of intervention?

2. What would you consider an appropriate mode of address to God in a prayer? How much does it matter?

12

Prayer – Part II

Our father in heaven, hallowed be your name. Your kingdom come. Your will be done, on earth as it is in heaven. Give us this day our daily bread. And forgive us our debts, as we also have forgiven our debtors. And do not bring us to the time of trial, but rescue us from the evil one.   (Matthew 6:9-13)

Liturgical events are times when beliefs are expressed, celebrated and reinforced. This is why we need to choose the content with such care. Remember the boys from Bandywallop (Chapter 4), going through their ritual in the dressing room before a game? What then do we think the content of prayers in liturgical events should be?

In Chapter 11 we said that God *hears* prayers but does not *answer* prayers – at least in the sense of some divine intervention. Some will ask 'What, then, is the point to saying prayers?' It seems to me that carefully saying prayers would be an exercise of great potential – even if there were **no** God! Why ever should I say that?

When I entered theological school there were two aspects of ministry in which I wanted to be proficient; namely, preaching and counselling. Preaching is not on our agenda until Chapter 13. But in respect of the latter I began at once to read greedily, to take subjects, to enrol in seminars and symposia, and clumsily (at first) to practice my rudimentary skills. One of the first books I read began by saying that the paramount requirement in counselling was to listen: to listen with close attention not only for what was being said but equally for what was *not* being said.

As an illustration of what is meant here, I often found that queries about what happens when we die were not about the after-life *per se*; they were related to an unresolved guilt or anxiety over some misdemeanour. That is to say, these queries were not really about the after-life except insofar as eternal punishment might be awaiting the sinner, and why one might dread that awaiting him/her if he/she had a guilty conscience. They would be wondering if there was an unforgivable sin!

I also clearly remember many occasions when 40-45 minutes went by with scarcely a word from me; when there was little more than a nod and a grunt, with perhaps the odd little acknowledgement like, "So, you have been feeling … etc." At the conclusion of a time like this, a troubled person could rise to leave saying, "Thank you so much. That really helped." In fact, I had said virtually nothing; all I had done was listen! What had helped was the opportunity this time gave the other to **name** what was bothering him/her. I discovered that this process was sometimes called 'catharsis', which comes from a Greek word for cleansing; it means getting stuff out of one's system. Of course, it doesn't mean full and permanent cure of the trouble, but often it seems to go a long way towards this.

My discovery was that 'naming' whatever is on one's mind is to an extent exercising some power over it – and reducing its power over us. Avoiding, bottling up, suppressing, refusing to acknowledge something, is counter-productive. So, where does this lead in thinking about the content of prayers? It gets me to the point where I see articulating things that make me feel glad, mad, sad or bad as being a whole lot better than never doing so.

First those things that make one feel **GLAD**. Some years ago, when I was preaching at St Michael's Uniting Church (Melbourne), my address contained an illustration about a woman whom I had told of an old Alexander's hymn that begins

> *When upon life's billows you are tempest tossed,*
> *When you are discouraged, thinking all is lost,*
> *Count your many blessings, name them one by one,*
> *And it will surprise you what the Lord hath done.*

I asked the organist to play the tune when I came to this point in the address and gave him a nod. It worked splendidly, but with one unintended consequence. In the hand-shaking afterwards, probably one-third of the congregation said, "Why didn't you let us sing it!" This was a song not in our hymnal, and which they had probably not sung since childhood; yet its message was embedded in their memories, and they wanted to sing it. Naming things that make us glad is good!

Every preacher has what are called 'travellers'; these are sermons or addresses delivered over and over, with small modifications to make them fit the occasion! My most travelled is called 'The Grace of Gratitude'; it has been heard from over seventy pulpits in England, the US, New Zealand, Fiji and most Australian states. It is a simple five-point message with good illustrations (which are what people remember!) on why being a thankful kind of person is a good thing for oneself and for everyone else. But thankfulness is empty of meaning unless it is focussed in concrete benefits and blessings for which we are genuinely glad, and unless these can be named without embarrassment. Furthermore, as I have suggested above, even if God were not to exist, there is much to be said for this 'grace of gratitude'.

The obverse is in *those things that make one feel* **MAD**; i.e. which are perplexing, confusing, daunting, frustrating because there does not seem to be any clear way to deal with them. What we need at such times is the ability to free up a little, to think clearly, to contact a spring of resources deep within, to trust our judgement and to say, "I can face this with equanimity."

Even if there were no God listening (but I think there is), it seems to me that such prayers enable us to name our demons and thereby exorcise them. Prayers of this type need not be encyclopaedic and exhausting (they often are); they may be better if they include good periods of quiet. I choose not to use the old-fashioned terms 'petition' and 'supplication' for such prayers because both tend to convey the idea of grovelling before some potentate.

Third, *those things that make one feel* **SAD**. Two highly-charged emotional crises quite commonly account for church 'alumni' (as Bishop Spong calls them) coming back for another try. One is concern for someone they love who is doing it hard, or concern for the way society seems to be going crazy. The other precipitating cause is some big 'stressor' like grief and loss of some sort, or some other personal trauma. Invariably one finds in a gathered congregation, or on the edge of that congregation, some people (maybe entire families) who are looking for consolation, comfort and courage. We should be constantly on the look-out for these people, who may be only occasional worshippers, but who have come on this day desperate. In my judgement they are the most important people there; never forget that!

I am all for thinking about victims of fire, flood and famine on the far side of the globe, but members of a congregation may be focussed on a nephew who has dropped out of school, a woman with a violent husband or an old lady who has been burgled – and wanting to see these people somehow find a good way through their situation. They are more inclined to 'name' these things than to name something that is remote from their lives. This also may be where times of silence are better than the congregation circling the globe in 8-10 minutes of verbosity or worse.

I turn now to *those things that make us feel **BAD***. This is a pivotal issue in how we think of ourselves in relation to God, and how we worship. One spring afternoon in 1968, when I was a village parson in New Hampshire (USA) my organist and choir director Ellen Sanborn and I were discussing the worship. She asked why I often began the service by telling God how low we were! I don't think I did, but that must have been her impression. As I recall, my answer was rather lame.

Fifteen or twenty years on, I was privy to a conversation with Robert Schuller, founder of the Crystal Cathedral in Los Angeles, whence emanated 'Hour of Power'. He was asked why there was no prayer of confession at the start of worship. "People come to church already bruised", he said. "It is not my intention to send them away more bruised than when they arrived!"

Another fifteen or twenty years on, I was at the induction of a minister to her new parish. We were all required to say at the start of the service, "We have been blind to the vision of a renewed world and deaf to your call to discipleship. We have been indifferent to the suffering of others and unwilling to forgive one another." Seated beside me was one of the first doctors who went into Changi prison camp in 1945 to assess and treat the inmates. He was to become one of our most respected and loved medicos, and was a teacher of two doctors in my family. I fumed. "How dare you," I mumbled, "making this beautiful human being demean himself with such mealy-mouthed rubbish!"

I have not said a prayer of 'confession' since that time. If others wish to do so, I cannot stop them. But I have been coming to the conclusion that this doctrine of sin, especially as developed by Augustine, is one of our most pernicious bestowments to the human race. In essence it is that all are born in a fallen state; there is a 'seminal' iniquity in every human being.

Today I repudiate this with the affirmation that there is a seminal goodness in every human being. OK, we do things that are ignorant, foolish and unkind; some of us do more of those things than others do. But this does not make us utterly depraved. We all do things that are carefully thought through, wise and kind; some of us do more of these than others do. But this does not make us saints either.

What I am contending for is another doctrine of humanity that says, 'in the heart of a person there is a drive and a will to goodness; not a will to do evil.' When we do evil, there are often clear reasons. I said recently to my wife that had I lived in the slums of London during the late 18th century, with a starving family and no work, I may well have been convicted for petty theft and come to this colony in chains! Often those who do what the rest of us disapprove are clearly affected by circumstances. That is not to excuse their actions, but to understand that in similar circumstances we could do the same.

But the doctrine of sin is a companion piece with the doctrine of salvation. It goes like this. We need a saviour because we are inherently sinful. Because we are inherently sinful we need a saviour. The church and its apparatchiks become the means by which we gain access to our saviour and to our salvation. Reminding us of our sinfulness has been in times past a powerful means for keeping people in check and for keeping them in thrall to bad religion.

The fact that it has worked so well for 2,000 years is no

justification for hanging on to this doctrine. Jesus did not come preaching sin and salvation, much less saying, "I am he by whose death you will be saved." Jesus came sharing his vision of the best possible world – which he called 'the kingdom of heaven', and inviting all and sundry to share in bringing this about.

The evidence we have suggests that those who thought themselves 'nobodies' were certainly not seen this way by Jesus. On the contrary, he encouraged men and women of all sorts to lay hold on the seminal goodness within them and let it work. He would show them how. Their 'possibilities' are implicit in the Sermon on the Mount. Had these possibilities not been realisable, his offering them as a way of life would have been a very unkind act. The distinguished Australian preacher Gordon Powell, explaining the choice of 'rough diamonds' in his birthday book, said,

> *"(But) Christianity is founded on the conviction there is a diamond in every soul no matter how rough the exterior. Every human being is capable of acting nobly at some time."*
>
> (Gordon Powell. *Famous Birthdays.* Melbourne: Joint Board of Christian Education, 1988. p.iii)

Of course, the truth is that all of us with any conscience are aware of doing things we shouldn't have done, and overlooking things we should have done. Sometimes this has been deliberate; often it is just plain carelessness. When it happens, someone is affected, and we know this (or should know it). I am not trying to skate away from that or even to offer what Dietrich Bonhoeffer called 'cheap grace'.

Experience with counselling seems to suggest that occasionally naming these events and/or times can be good for the soul; certainly better than trying to avoid or suppress them. It can be healing to hear that we need not stay in a place that makes us feel bad, but can move on. In the place of a prayer of confession, the liturgical event could well begin with a leader declaring these five affirmations and all responding with a hearty 'Amen!'

- We are surrounded and filled with the sacred presence. AMEN!
- We are not victims of our past. AMEN!

- We can forgive ourselves and others. AMEN!
- We have our own strengths and abilities. AMEN!
- We have something good to offer the world. AMEN!

One of the worst features of traditional protestant worship has surely been the so-called 'pastoral' prayer, frequently characterised by its inordinate length. On a visit to Melbourne sixty years ago, Dr Leslie Weatherhead of London's City Temple (Congregational) likened this prayer to a round-the-world trip in a high flying spiritual aeroplane. He explained that some time into the journey, the passengers begin one-by-one to fall out. They try to catch up and follow on foot, but soon realise this is fruitless and settle down to await the plane's return. Having circumnavigated the globe, it arrives back carrying the pilot alone – and passengers reboard in time to say 'Amen'.

This was a sardonic observation on the worst excesses of wordiness. Of course, the loquacious in (largely protestant) prayer meetings have been known to match this. Both clergy and lay persons seem prone to forgetting those words that precede the Lord's Prayer in the gospel according to Matthew. "When you are praying, do not heap up empty phrases as the gentiles do; for they think they will be heard because of their many words." (Matthew 6:7) I have listened to marathon offerings from lay members assigned the 'prayers for others' on Sunday mornings and wondered if they were not seeking to outdo each other!

There is another characteristic about which the less is said, the better. I call it liturgical sadism: the use of prayer as a weapon for assaulting the mute and defenceless (rather like the prayers of confession dealt with above). Visiting a place known for its conservatism, I was nonetheless taken aback when a brother rose to offer prayer after my address. The prayer contained phrases like 'faithless interpreters', 'true to your holy word', 'deliverance from false prophets' and so on. I left quickly that morning! Prayers should not be 'accusatory' or even 'hortatory'. They should help the hearers speak with and listen to God. They are definitely not an alternative type of preaching!

QUESTIONS FOR THOUGHT AND TALK

1. What experiences, if any, can you recall of prayers that seemed to be rather too long – or even excessively long?

2. Discuss the 'menu' of topics suggested for prayer under glad, mad, sad and bad. Anything important left out?

13

Preaching???

"And the large crowd was listening to him with delight" (Mark 12:37)

During the 90s a number of younger ministers urged me to set down in a book what I had learned about the art of preaching. When *Excited to Speak, Exciting to Hear* was released in 2003 one former student said, "Best thing I've read on the subject; only one thing wrong with it." I invited him to elaborate. "Twenty years too late!"

I wish he were wrong, but I fear he is not. I see little evidence today among ministers of any hunger for real excellence as communicators. I see little evidence of their being 'excited to speak', and even less of their being considered 'exciting to hear'. Does this mean that preaching may now be considered passé? I have certainly heard so.

Yet, as I telegraphed in Chapter 1 (*Bored Silly*), one of the biggest and fastest growing industries is the manufacture and delivery of monologues; talking at conferences, conventions, seminars and dinners. A glance at the internet indicates that we have at least 3,000 speakers registered with one or other agency, and ready to deliver their *entertaining, motivating and inspirational* addresses for any type of audience, at fees ranging between $5,000 and $20,000.

Do preachers see themselves called to deliver *entertaining, motivating and inspirational* addresses? I would have to say there is very little evidence of this. On the contrary, it would appear that most feel anointed to make sure that nobody is entertained, motivated or inspired – if one is to infer anything from the product. Congregations must accept some culpability in this matter – for they have quietly rolled over during the last three decades and resigned themselves to being bored. At another time they may have confronted their preachers, but not these days.

So it was that after drafting an outline for *Excited to Speak, Exciting to Hear* over Easter 1995, I lost heart and dropped the project. I was even then coming reluctantly to the conclusion that the pursuit of excellence in pulpits was just a distant memory. Then in 2000 I sat in the lounge room of Australia's most notable preacher – Dr Gordon Powell, who at one time had preached every Wednesday to 750,000 Australians, courtesy the Macquarie radio network. Gordon scolded me for losing heart, and said, "I want you to get back to it. And I will help you!" I was caught, and duly resumed the task. He read and critiqued every chapter, and then wrote a most generous foreword. It begins with this statement:

> *"No calling has so changed human history as that of the preacher. Take out Jesus, Peter, Paul, Mohammed, Buddha, Confucius, Luther, Calvin, Knox, Wesley – to name only some who spring to mind – and history would be unrecognisable. Every time we write the date we honour the greatest preacher of all. A return to dynamic preaching would bring untold blessing. That is why this book is so important."*
>
> (John Bodycomb. *Excited to Speak, Exciting to Hear: The Art of Preaching.* Adelaide: Openbook Publishers, 2003. p.i)

Whether or not Gordon Powell's confident prediction will ever be embraced, it seems to me that the onus of proof rests with those who would claim that preaching is passé; who try to argue that there is no place in the liturgical event for a 'message' that is entertaining, inspirational and motivating!

None of the foregoing is an apologia for 20-minute or 30-minute sermons being returned to liturgical events in Evolving Christianity. However, it is a rebuttal of the nonsensical claim that monologues have no place – anywhere! That is a self-justifying untruth promoted by those who lack any commitment to excellence as communicators; also by resigned congregations who no longer expect this and whose silence signifies consent to mediocrity!

The decision on whether a high-class 'homily' of 7, 12 or 18 minutes should be a feature of worship in Evolving Christianity must be made by the people in conjunction with their leader(s). My own view is that some input of this kind is important, but it should not be regarded as a pedagogical tool. The sanctuary is not a classroom. It is this mistaken idea which may help to account for the decline; i.e., preaching becoming at best an exercise in dull didactic instruction and at worst downright soporific.

QUESTIONS FOR THOUGHT AND TALK

1. Discuss the author's judgement on the decline of preaching. Insofar as he is correct, what might account for this?

2. Do you think there is a role for the EIM (entertaining, inspirational and motivating) 'message' in Evolving Christian worship?

PART III
OUTCOMES

14

Putting it together

*"Those who wait upon the Lord shall renew their
strength, they shall mount up with wings like eagles,
they shall run and not be weary, they shall walk and
not faint" (Isa. 40:31)*

Yes, we know that! We have heard it many times as an opening 'call
to worship', but it doesn't seem to work that easily. Maybe this
'waiting upon the Lord' needs to be re-examined and re-worked a
bit. What is it exactly that we are trying to achieve, any way?

In his *Introduction to Christian Worship* (1981) James White said,
"worship itself is an exasperatingly difficult word to pin down." I
imagine that once we move from the simplistic definition like 'going
to church, singing hymns and saying prayers', we are likely to be in
hearty agreement with Professor White – but that is no reason for
giving up.

What do the 'consumers' think it is all about? Suffice to say, there
are very different notions of worship, and very different expectations.
When we look at these it is possible to discern three clearly distinct
'emphases'. If you imagine a hollow triangle, full of little dots
representing people, there will be concentrations of dots toward each
corner of the triangle, and a spread of dots in and around the centre
of it. What are the three corners of this triangle?

First, to some people worship is predominantly **a celebration of
some kind of community**. It is a place and a happening in which
differences and disagreements are transcended. They might even
allude to the story of Pentecost in Acts Chapter 2 – which recounts

how barriers dropped away between people of different racial, cultural and religious background. They would probably remind us that worship has a 'horizontal' dimension as well as a vertical one; that it is the act of a community, whose sense of community must be continually renewed in the celebration. People like this are apt to prefer the 'worship in the round' spatial arrangement, and also a fair degree of informality. They don't mind plenty of chit-chat; even the passing of the peace getting a bit chaotic!

Second, to others worship is predominantly **a way of access to renewal of the flagging spirit.** Some of them will use an expression like 'recharging your battery'. To them, worship should somehow point people to ways of dealing with pressing fears, problems and needs. They remind us that worship is the 'interface' between human need and God's action. However, if the emphasis is so solemnly on God's mighty acts that it fails to speak meaningfully to human need, they may go away hungry. They like sermons about fear, anxiety, grief, loneliness, stress – that speak to the human condition.

Third, to others again worship is predominantly **an acknowledgement of transcendence.** To them it should pivot on the might, majesty and dynamic activity of God – and provide a context for suitably registering praise, adoration and homage to the highest of which they can conceive. They remind us that worship should not be allowed to slip into mere contemplation of human existence, with somewhat introverted hymns, prayers and preaching. (Some call this 'navel-gazing!')

The three positions described here do not have to be mutually exclusive or contradictory; they are more matters of emphasis. In the triangle some people would position themselves very firmly at one corner or another, while others would consider themselves equidistant from all three corners. I am not about to say anyone in this triangle is more 'right' than anyone else; only that in designing any kind of liturgical event, it is perhaps wise to remember this diversity of expectations. I incline personally toward the idea of trying to get one's mind off oneself and centred on the sacred, and (perhaps because I am old!) I like some dignity and decorum. More anon on what my individual preference would be!

In her classic simply called *Worship* the distinguished Anglo-Catholic mystic and writer Evelyn Underhill (1875-1941) set down one of the more helpful of formal definitions; it is helpful because it does not rule out everyone bar the Christians. It is a very 'inclusive' definition.

Underhill said, "worship is an acknowledgement of Transcendence; that is to say, of a Reality independent of the worshipper, which is always more or less deeply coloured by mystery, and which is there first." This definition can be applicable to a wide variety of liturgical activities, to a wide variety of people and probably most religions.

It is close to the way I understand Worship. I use the term to mean, quite simply, *concentrating with intent* on the Other (with a capital 'O'). I do not concentrate on God 24 hours of the day; not at all. However, that does not mean the relationship with God is discontinued. If I use the metaphor of a relationship, then it is probably correct to say that any relationship is at its best when there are times and ways of concentrating on the other.

At the human level, special times of concentrating on the other (in whatever ways we do it) are what keep any relationship at its best. It is quaint that the old Anglican order for marriage said, "With my body I thee worship, with all my worldly goods I thee endow." I take 'with my body … &c' to denote physical intimacy – when one is uniquely aware of and attentive to the other. One does not 'worship' the other like this all day and every day, but in what modern parlance has called 'quality times'.

And so, my own term for what worship is all about is *Awareness and Attentiveness*. As should have been clear from Parts I and II, in my view there can be no single, God-given, eternal and unchangeable way this should happen. There are many different ways, and if they help us in becoming more deeply aware and more deeply attentive, then they are good and laudable.

But there still remains the question: is there any kind of basis on which a group of people might put together a liturgical event that is both worthy of the One they worship and worthwhile activity for them? On a morning walk last year, with not another person to be seen, I had what I suppose was a kind of 'waking dream'. In my imagination it was as though I met Rabbi Jesus, who was also out for a morning walk! When I got home I wrote down as accurately as I could what I remembered. What follows is my account of this. I called it

An appointment with the Guru from Galilee as an allegory for worship, and as a guide to designing a liturgical event.

1. I have heard about the Guru from Galilee, and when he is pointed out to me, I approach him to request a conversation.

2. He sees me walking towards him; with a smile, a wave and a word of welcome encourages me to approach.

3. I do this with the appropriate courtesies one customarily gives to one who deserves special respect.

4. He comes quickly to the point. "What ails you? I heard you were wishing to speak." I tell him it has not been a very good week.

5. "You need not be mired in the past," he says. "You can recover from stumbles and make a new start. Leave it behind you."

6. That, I would say, is a good word for anyone; i.e. assurance that I can begin again! "Were you wanting something more of me?"

7. "Indeed I was, Rabbi," say I. "I wanted to ask how you would counsel a man like me on the art of living."

8. He says, "Do you read the scriptures?" "Now and again, Rabbi." "Then you may remember that our prophet Isaiah says …"

9. Then follows this exquisite little story that encapsulates something Isaiah said. But now others are gathering, and want his attention.

10. "Thank you, Rabbi," I say. "I shall take what you have shown me and seek to live according to it."

11. "Blessings on you," he says. "Set some priorities now, lest the message be lost."

It seemed to me that this little chat suggested four main steps in a conversation with 'G-O-D' (who, after all, we believe to be somehow apparent in Jesus). These steps are

- From 1, 2 and 3 an act of 'focussing' on G-O-D; saying "Hello"!
- From 4, 5 and 6 an acknowledgement of bruises sustained and bruises inflicted; dumping needless baggage.
- From 6, 7, 8 and 9 a period of attending to G-O-D for illumination.
- From 10 and 11 a response to what has been heard.

Perhaps rather surprisingly, I actually quite like a liturgical event that could seem to some people rather 'traditional' in its form. In the following outline, which grows out of what I have said above, there are places for music, but no spaces where hymns are specified. It will be noted that neither is there a place in this very basic order for the sacrament of bread and wine. This may or may not be a part of the event, but as a 'non-conformist', I do not find it mandatory.

(Musical prelude for settling the mind and helping 'focus')

Very short call to worship, to aid in focussing
Prayer about healing of hurts sustained and hurts caused
Three to four minutes of silence
Word of Healing (i.e., about being forgiven and forgiving)
Readings from scripture AND other literature (by skilled lector)

(Music to facilitate 'openness' to new light and truth)

Homily of seven or eight minutes
Three to four minutes of silence
Expressions of concern for others (including significant silences)
Dismissal

(Musical postlude)

Frankly, I can see no persuasive argument for writing *new* calls to worship, *new* opening prayers, *new* offertory prayers, *new* dismissals &c every single week. The attempt to do this can often result in some mediocre mass-produced products. In fact, there is a constant stream of mediocre material available on the internet. It may be better to focus our creative energies on constructing one of each type of prayer, perhaps varied according to the season of the community's life.

The words do not have to be flamboyant, extravagant, pietistic; better if they are not. They should be simple, elegant and dignified – like the classic collect for purity in the Anglican tradition, which I find one of the most elegant prayers written. Ponder its 43 words

> *Almighty God unto whom all hearts be open, all desires known*
> *and from whom no secrets are hid: cleanse the thoughts of our*
> *hearts by the inspiration of thy Holy Spirit that we may perfectly*
> *love thee and worthily magnify thy holy name.*

Expressions of concern for others can also follow a similar format each time, although naturally the content will vary. Chapter 15 provides some illustrations of this.

QUESTIONS FOR THOUGHT AND TALK

1. Discuss the expression 'Awareness and Attentiveness' as a definition of what Worship is about? Feel free to improve on it.

2. Discuss the outline on pages 86-87 for designing a liturgical event. Do you see any deficiencies or defects in it?

15

How One People Prayed

This chapter contains a random selection of Sunday prayers from St Aidan's Uniting Church, North Balwyn (Victoria), which I prepared and led during a two-year period as 'minister in association'. Some weeks I took up to a half-hour writing the opening prayer! Prayers for Others were never completed before Sunday morning, because they grew out of the 'news' items.

The prayers do not pretend to be 'avant-garde', but they *are* different. Opening Prayers are intended to help people centre on the Mystery of God and to feel at their ease in that centering – not striving after or for anything, but simply acknowledging this great reality around them and within. They would first have said the responsive litany that starts "In the beginning was God" (Chapter 16). There are no prayers of 'adoration' or of 'confession'. This is because the first hymn can be expected to express something like adoration more than adequately. The absence of 'confession' is explained in Chapter 12.

The Offering Prayers are an attempt to capture and express something for which the people would be genuinely grateful – and as such, moved to respond somehow. What of the Prayers for Others? These are commonly one of the great 'messy' areas of worship, especially when assigned to members of a congregation, who are inclined to wax more eloquent than is necessary. The features, every Sunday, of these prayers for others at St Aidan's were as follows:

1. There were commonly three major foci for prayer. The third almost always had to do with members of the congregation in special need, but how this was done is explained below.

2. The topics were often briefly introduced, and there was sometimes also a word about what we were doing when praying for others.

3. Three periods of silence (not less than 30 seconds) were important. The people became quickly accustomed to these, which were concluded with the ringing of a bell plus versicle and response.
4. This time of prayer always concluded with the Lord's Prayer, said fairly slowly and thoughtfully.

In the time when attention was on members of the congregation, names were never mentioned. Instead, there was reference to 'members and friends of this congregation' –

"looking for a good way to exercise their gifts in the world"
"who have felt pushed close to their limits"
"seeking something positive and strengthening to embrace"
"drawing little or no help from the faith they've held"
"facing hard decisions and unsure what is right"
"who have been too long under too much stress"
"grieving over recent losses, or anticipating imminent losses"
"who face daunting challenges"
"facing threats to health or other things that sorely test them"
"who feel they've little left for facing hard times"

The choice of words commonly grew out of ministers' conversations during the week with or about members of the congregation, or with their friends and relatives. That is to say, the words didn't come out of nowhere. There was always a specificity about them, but without individuals or households being named. This allowed members of the congregation to insert into the prayer the identity of those who came to mind.

There are two issues in respect of naming individuals or households. One is the matter of privacy. It is appropriate to mention names *only* with the explicit request or approval of the person(s) named. Details, of course, would not be announced. The other consideration is that naming can *exclude* (or sound like excluding) from the prayer those who are not named, and so inadvertently give hurt to someone.

If there is a widespread and strong wish for individuals and/or households to be named, this can be done by reading a list before the prayer time and saying, "When we think of members and friends, we will have especially in mind today the following people."

St Aidan's Prayers   24.2.08

After a brief word of welcome to visitors
and the litany ("In the beginning was God")

Opening Prayer

The presence of the Sacred is around us and within us. God, let us
be more and more deeply aware of this, in wonder and in gratitude.
Let us be more and more deeply aware of the great forces that can
be unleashed within us – for the calming of anxiety, for the forgiving
of faults, for the renewing of hopes and for power to make a
difference in the world. We claim the promises, in the spirit of Jesus.
Amen.

Offering Prayer

God, we are glad to be part of this household of faith and we want
to spread what we have found here. Toward that end we make our
offerings, in the spirit of Jesus. *Amen.*

Prayers for Others

In the prayers for others we first put ourselves in the way of God's
blessings for people of faith – laying hold on those great positive
energies that renew love and hope and serenity and courage in the
human spirit; then we offer these as gifts to those for whom we pray.
We say "*These are for you.*" Three topics this morning: young people
resuming studies and already registering stress, those concerned about
wild nights in our city, those who have lost loved ones in the week
just past. Now we focus …

- Young people resuming study and encountering stress need
  and deserve supporting prayer. (silence) Lord, you hear us.
  Lord, you hear our prayer.
- Police and others acknowledging anxiety over wild and
  violent behaviour in the city at night need and deserve
  supporting prayer. (silence) Lord, you hear us. *Lord, you hear*
  our prayer.
- Those known to us who have lost loved ones and are in grief,
  need and deserve supporting prayer. (silence) Lord, you hear
  us. *Lord, you hear our prayer.*

We have prayed as Jesus would have prayed, and say *Our Father* …

St Aidan's Prayers   25.5.08

After a brief word of welcome to visitors
and the litany ("In the beginning was God")

Opening Prayer

God, we have careered in here with much clutter and clamour and commotion crowding our heads, and wanting to clear it away that we might truly hear the whispers of your Spirit. We believe you are speaking softly, and so we will try to listen attentively in the way of Jesus. *Amen.*

Offering Prayer

God, we make these offerings to help assure the ever-widening ripples of influence emanating from this place, in the spirit of Jesus. *Amen.*

Prayers for Others

Last week, in the prayers for others, some of you were deeply aware of the surging love and practical concern generated when an entire congregation is focussed. It is a time when good energies are released in the lives of those we pray for, and of those who work with them. This morning we pray for World Vision staff and other aid workers in Myanmar and China. We pray for the 20,000 young people homeless every night in Australia, and for those working with them. We pray for members of this faith community, and those near to them, where courage is needed in the face of adversity. Now let us focus …

- World Vision staff and other aid workers in Myanmar and China with cyclone and earthquake victims, need and deserve supporting prayer. (silence) Lord, you hear us. *Lord, you hear our prayer.*
- The 20,000 young people in Australia homeless every night, and those who seek to relieve that situation, need and deserve supporting prayer. (silence) Lord, you hear us. *Lord, you hear our prayer.*
- Members of this faith community, and those near to them, whose courage is flagging in the face of adversity need and deserve supporting prayer. Lord, you hear us. *Lord, you hear our prayer.*

We bring these prayers as Jesus would have prayed; *Our Father* …

St Aidan's Prayers   30.11.08

After a brief word of welcome to visitors
and the litany ("In the beginning was God")

Opening Prayer

As we have just reminded ourselves, *God is around us and within.* Good
Spirit, we look for a deeper awareness of this, and for the outcomes
from it: a composure within, a commitment to live fully and a
compassion for our fellow humans. We want to be the best that we
can be, as was the passion of Jesus. This is our prayer. *Amen.*

Offering Prayer

We are glad for what we have, and sad for those with little or none.
May our offerings today help to make the world more just and fair,
according to the wish and the ways of Jesus. *Amen.*

Prayers for Others

We take time to think of those who need every help they can get.
But first, a quiet moment to claim the good presence around us and
within. (silence) We focus on three groups.

- Arabs and Jews, with much pain and anger from dispossession
  of land, yet hoping for a peaceful accord, need and deserve
  supporting prayer (silence) Lord, you hear us. *Lord, you hear
  our prayer.*
- Young families anxious about child care facilities, and the staff
  of these centres, need and deserve supporting prayer. (silence)
  Lord, you hear us. *Lord, you hear our prayer.*
- Members and friends of this congregation, carrying wounds
  of spirit that are slow to heal, need and deserve supporting
  prayer. (silence) Lord, you hear us. *Lord, you hear our prayer.*

We bring these concerns as followers of him who taught us we
could say *Our Father ...*

I cannot emphasise too strongly that none of these prayer segments
in the liturgy were 'rushed'. The style of delivery was slow without
being ponderous, reverent without being sanctimonious, thoughtful
without being dead-slow.

The feature of them all that allowed for people to think their way
through with the leader is my obsession with *economy of words*! I make

no apology for this. The three prayers I most deeply love are the Lord's Prayer (54 words), the Collect for Purity (43 words) and the so-called 'serenity prayer' of Reinhold Niebuhr (35 words).

QUESTIONS FOR THOUGHT AND TALK

1. Discuss critically the form and length of the 'Opening Prayers'. In your judgement would they help worshippers centre in the Sacred? Do you find the lack of Adoration and Confession a shortcoming?

2. What do you think we are doing with prayers of intercession (i.e. the Prayers for Others)? Does this form of intercession achieve what you want from such prayers? What would you change?

16

Litanies and Prayers

Although there are many superb collections of prayers, these are best taken as 'resources' for those who are shaping liturgical events. I have benefited greatly from reading the prayers of others, including from traditions other than Christian. However, I prefer to write my own and encourage those who seek appropriate ways of worship in Evolving Christianity to write their own.

What follows here is simply a random assortment of items I have written over recent years, for a variety of uses. The first of them, 'For the start of worship' was intended for only *one* Sunday at St Aidan's, but it came to be used over and over; this may be because it encapsulates rather well just about everything Evolving Christianity needs to embrace!

FOR THE START OF WORSHIP

V. In the beginning was God –
R. the source of all that is.
V. By God all is sustained;
R. without God nothing could be.

V. Humanity duly came –
R. to enjoy and care for the earth;
V. to live in peace and accord
R. as one great family.

V. Jesus came from God –
R. to show us true humanity.
V. We gather to celebrate this faith
R. and to listen for the Eternal Voice.

All. The Spirit is around us and within.
Praise to the Eternal Spirit.

OPENING SENTENCES FOR WORSHIP

These words may be used in a variety of ways:
as 'calls to worship', as prayers, as responsive litanies.

As oxygen is around us and within
and without it we would not be,
so God is around us and within
and without God we would not be.
As deliberate deep breaths
are good for the body,
so with deep breathing of the Spirit
we call God.
Think of worship and prayer
as such deep breathing.
Let it renew your love of life.

People gather in this place
to bathe in the healing springs we call God.
They come with hurts and bruises –
some caused by others,
some by circumstance,
some self-inflicted.
Whatever the cause,
they can find healing here
in the love that brought all into being
and holds it in being.

If you seek a richer connection
with the energies that hold
the universe in being,
a lifting of your spirit
and a renewal of your strength,
this is a good place to be.
In this hour,
affirm your connectedness with God,
in the deeps of your being –
and let that be renewing.

A PRAYER FOR START OF LITURGY

Eternal Mystery of many names,
for whom each of us has a favourite,
we address you by that name
knowing that you hear us.

Now we seek to hear you
in the holy whispers,
and to respond
to the inner promptings –

as Jesus did.

This is our prayer.
AMEN

A LETTING GO PRAYER

Eternal Mystery of many names,
we have come with burdens
we need to lay down:
where we have been hurt
or hurt others,
where we have made mistakes
and need to move on.

You invite us to lay down burdens
and to move on.
we claim that promise

as Jesus would.

This is our prayer.
AMEN

FIRST SECTION OF A LITURGICAL EVENT

Leader says: God is the surrounding, saturating sacred presence
in whom dwells everything and everyone.
who indwells everything and everyone,
who envelops and infuses all that is.
God is in all and all is in God.

All say: We gather to sense this more deeply;
to listen more intently,
to respond more heartily,
to the Eternal Mystery.

Focussing Prayer (all say)

We would still our minds;
be free of distraction,
more conscious of the holy
around us and within,
attentive and ready to respond.
This is our prayer. AMEN.

Healing Prayer (all say)

We have sustained hurt
both accidental and intended,
and need to forgive.
We have inflicted hurt
both accidental and intended,
and need to be forgiven.
We look for the strong impulse
to forgive and for the humility
to accept forgiveness.
This is our prayer. AMEN

Leader says: God says, Whatever the damage on you
and on the other, new beginnings can be made.

All say: We are glad and grateful.

QUESTIONS FOR THOUGHT AND TALK

1. Can you compose a 'focussing' or 'centring' prayer, and also a 'healing' prayer of not more than about forty words in each case, and share this with others in your group?

2. Some like having a printed order for a liturgical event; some don't. Discuss the pros and cons of having a printed order.

17

Rites of Passage

When I came into faith at the age of 19 my first Christian book was *Letters to Young Churches*, a version of the New Testament epistles in modern English. The translator was Anglican priest John Bertram Phillips (1906-1982). Serving in London during World War II, Phillips was saddened to find his young people could make no sense of the Bible. He began by paraphrasing the letter to the Colossians while waiting in air raid shelters during the Blitz. My nutriment as a young Christian was this correspondence – *in words that I spoke*!

At 25 I was launched into broadcasting on local radio – sometimes up to five days a week. These little talks were called 'thoughts for the day' or 'epilogues' depending on whether they were early morning or late evening. The idea was to translate the categories of Christian thought into terms that made easy and helpful listening for all – regardless of religious affiliation or none. And so, for over 60 years I have looked for alternative ways to talk about faith and life. Involvement with Evolving Christianity has given added impetus to something with which I have, therefore, been much longer engaged.

The challenge to aim for this is never more exciting than in baptisms, weddings and funerals. In these three 'rites of passage' one is dealing with a disparate collection of human beings, many of whom will not be seen again until the next baptism, wedding or funeral. Some of them will have residual Christian memory, and some will have none of this.

With such people, our strict adherence to a prescribed order is apt to be bewildering at best, if not downright unintelligible. The familiar verbiage may sound 'lovely' to older folks but daggy to the young. The fact that their presence is a great challenge and opportunity to *interpret* faith coherently is not always fully appreciated by clergy. The first of these occasions is the baptism of infants, which is still frequently requested by parents who have only the most tenuous links with church life. Thus, something like this ...

BAPTISM

"Hi. Is that the reverend?" "That's right. Andrew Stone here. Can I be of help?" "We want to get Michael Jackson done." "You want to talk about Michael's baptism?" "We all got done as kids, and Mum says we should organise it for him." "Right, sounds like a lovely thing to do for Michael. You're Mrs Jackson?" "No, that's his first names – Michael Jackson." "Oh. I didn't get your name." "You want mine or his dad's? We've got different names, see." "Yours will be fine. Who am I talking to?" "Gloria-Jean. Call me 'Gee-Jay' if you want; everyone else does."

This conversation is not atypical, and it can put some clergy in a minor spin. Should I bend over backwards to show 'Gee-Jay', her spouse and their infant that God's love is indiscriminate, or do I consider how this further erodes (corrodes?) what purists would call the given gospel? If we proceed to baptise Michael Jackson – and do this in the context of our regular service – how do we mediate the tension between gospel inclusiveness and 'cheap grace', as Dietrich Bonhoeffer called it? Even if there's a deep-and-meaningful or two with the young parents and we baptise Michael Jackson, what sort of wording can we employ that won't be gobbledegook to grandparents, godparents, uncles, aunts and other hangers-on?

What follows is the 'essence' of what needs to be said, always remembering that for Michael Jackson's baptism to be honoured by other Christian traditions, we need to use the words in Matthew 28:19!

What Baptism Means

We speak of God with caution. This is because God is beyond our understanding and our words. Yet Jesus spoke comfortably of God as *like* a loving parent. This is how we say *Our Father* with confidence.

We believe God brought the universe into being as a loving act; God wanted company. And so, we believe God loves the universe as we love our children – because we have 'pro-created' them by the power God gives us. God's love is not something people have to earn. It is a free gift, like the love of every good parent for his or her child.

Churches have customs called 'sacraments' that remind us of God's love. One is the holy meal; what we variously call the mass, the eucharist, communion, the lord's supper. The other is the holy bathing, mostly done symbolically by sprinkling of water.

This can be for adults or infants. Adults make their own decision for baptism. Infants receive it at their parents' request. Both 'sacraments' remind us that we belong to the Source of all being and of all love.

Scripture

(if Baptism not in context of public worship)

Reflection

(as above)

To the Parents

Do you request this sacrament for your son/daughter? **We do.**
Does Jesus reveal truths about God and about life for you? **He does.**
Will you try to help your son/daughter to know these truths. **We will.**

To the Godparents

Will you support the parents in their faith and resolve? **We will.**

To Others Present

Will all seek to support the parents in their faith and resolve? **We will.**

Gather around the baptismal font for

The Baptism

(making sure to say the formula in Matthew 28:19)

The Prayer

Good Spirit, around and within everything that is, we know you made everything as an act of love, that you are with your creation as one who encourages it to be the best it can be, and that we see this in Jesus. Make these truths real again in the sacrament of baptism, for all here and especially for .... (child's name). May he/she live life to the fullest, showing your likeness in the way Jesus does. This is our prayer. AMEN.

The Baptismal Candle

The Blessing and Dismissal

★★★★★

MARRIAGE

Most of the firmly non-religious who want a wedding ceremony will go to civil celebrants. Some will ask their mothers to have a word with some clergyperson she has heard about for his/her 'flexibility'. Hence one is apt to have a 'phone call that goes rather like this. "You won't know me, but I went to Sunday school at your church. My name is Shelley Beech – Mrs Beech." "To what do I owe the pleasure of your call, Mrs Beech?" "My husband and I were wondering if you would consider doing a wedding for our Sandy." "I don't see why not. Tell me a little more, though."

It turns out that Sandy and her partner have been cohabiting for two years, saving madly to pay off a house, variously sleeping and socialising on week-ends, and they're in church only for the occasional wedding, funeral or 'christening' as Mrs Beech calls it. Neither is hostile to organised religion; they're just not interested. When her parents say that a church wedding would be 'nice', Sandy says "You find us a church and we'll look at it." That is how Mrs Beech calls on the minister at the place where she went to Sunday school.

The minister, if she/he is willing and able, probably says that it's time for Sandy and her partner to arrange their own appointment – and proceeds to set up a series of them. But if he/she has some acquaintance with Evolving Christianity, what should go into the ceremony? One option is for it to be in traditionally and richly elegant 'prayer book' language, which some may love even though it sounds archaic. Another is to develop a form for marriage that is not inelegant, but that is contemporary and congruent with the kind of Christianity the minister espouses.

What *is* important is that marriage is appreciated as a social institution that existed before we did, and will exist after we have gone. It is *not* a purely 'private' contract (as it appears to be in many a civil ceremony!) This being the case, it could go something like the following. Not all of this wording would be appropriate if parties were of the same gender.

What Marriage Means

(Minister says) Life as we know it, in its emergence, takes the form of male and female. In the experience of humanity, life comes to fruition in the most intimate of relationships, typified by marriage. This ancient social institution is not merely for the regulating of conduct, but is the proven ground of continuing growth and fulfilment. And so, culture and religion alike give the seal of approval to the concept of marriage.

It is the wish of ...... and ...... to make public their commitment to each other and to the values, hopes and dreams they share. It is their belief that a partnership should be enriching to both, and should enhance their joint input to the common good; they wish to leave the world better for their having been a part of it. What unites them is in essence what all great faiths, including Christianity, say of marriage.

Accordingly, we are invited to hear words of wisdom on the matter – from the mystical writer and artist Kahlil Gibran and in the Hebrew and Christian scriptures.

Some Readings

From *The Prophet*★

Then Almitra spoke again and said …
"And what of Marriage, master?"
And he answered saying:
You were born together,
and together you shall be forevermore.
You shall be together when the white wings
of death scatter your days.
Aye, you shall be together even in the
silent memory of God.
But let there be spaces in your togetherness,
and let the winds of the heavens dance between you.
Love one another, but make not a bond of love.
Let it rather be a moving sea
between the shores of your souls.
Fill each other's cup but drink not from one cup.
Give one another of your bread but eat not from the same loaf.
Sing and dance together and be joyous,
but let each of you be alone,
even as the strings of a lute are alone
though they quiver with the same music.
Give your hearts, but not into each other's keeping.
For only the hand of Life can contain your hearts.
And stand together, yet not too near together.
For the pillars of the temple stand apart,
and the oak tree and the cypress
grow not in each other's shadow.

From Song of Songs 8:6-7

Set me as a seal upon your heart,
As a seal upon your arm;
For love is strong as death,
Passion fierce as the grave.
Its flashes are flashes of fire,

A raging flame.
Many waters cannot quench love,
Neither can floods drown it.
If one offered for love
All the wealth of his house,
It would be utterly scorned.

From I Corinthians 13:4-8
Love is patient,
Love is kind;
Love is not envious
Or boastful
Or arrogant
Or rude.
It does not insist on its own way;
It is not irritable or resentful;
It does not rejoice in wrongdoing,
But rejoices in the truth.
It bears all things,
Hopes all things
Endures all things.
Love never ends.

Declaration of Intent

Minister: We have been reminded of the meaning of marriage, in words inspired and inspiring. With this understanding, ... , do you intend to give yourself to ...... to be her husband, for life? **I DO**

And ......, do you intend to give yourself to ...... to be his wife, for life? **I DO**

Affirmation by the People

Minister: Will you, the families and friends of ...... and ......, uphold them in their marriage? **WE WILL**

The Vows

(vows must be clear and unambiguous to be legal)

Groom says: I ...... receive you ...... to be my wife. With your help I set myself to grow in those graces that will make me a better partner. I promise my love, loyalty and support. I will stand by you in all circumstances, as long as we live. This is my solemn vow.

Bride says: I ...... receive you ...... to be my husband. With your help I set myself to grow in those graces that will make me a better partner. I promise you my love, loyalty and support. I will stand by you in all circumstances, as long as we live. This is my solemn vow.

The Giving of Rings

As a circle is without beginning or ending,
so with the infinite love of the Eternal.
From love the universe was born;
in love it is sustained.
By love it is redeemed and renewed.
To reflect that love in life together
is the prayer of this man and this woman.
To symbolise their hope and aspiration,
the circles of gold, without beginning or ending.

Groom says: ......, I give you this ring as a sign of my promise, for all to see.

Bride says: ......, I give you this ring as a sign of my promise, for all to see.

Proclamation of Marriage

Minister says: Your life is given to you. You neither sought nor generated it yourselves. When life is spent with and for others, it is enhanced. You have committed yourselves to each other in the bond of marriage, and I now declare that you are husband and wife.

(people may wish to applaud)

Prayer and Blessing

Minister says: There can be a fine line between what some call 'prayer' and what others call 'thoughtful reflection', 'solemn hope' or 'a new resolve'. When these are directed to an Ultimate whom we name 'God', they are called 'prayer'. We recognise that for some this will be appropriate, but not necessarily for others. However, that need not preclude you from embracing the thoughts and meanings. Feel free to say a hearty 'Amen' at the end. Now, the prayer.

- Source of all that is, giver of our being and of all that makes it worthwhile, we declare our gratitude for the experience of loving and being loved.
- We rejoice with ...... and ...... in the making of this marriage. We want them to have the strength to keep their promises, to be loyal and faithful to each other, and to support each other.
- Let their hearts be constantly replenished with the love that bears all things, hopes all things, endures all things. This is our prayer. AMEN.

Now to the One in whom the universe was conceived, by whom it came to be and is held in being, who is the source of all that draws us away from futility and towards fulfilment, we commit each other. Go in peace. **AMEN.**

Gibran, Kahlil. *The Prophet*: **1923.**
Kahlil Gibran (1883–1931), Lebanese artist and writer, was a Maronite Christian. This work was largely unknown until 'discovered' in the 1960s by the US counterculture, whence I came by it in 1968. I believe I was the first to offer it to an Australian wedding couple (1970) for discussion and duly for inclusion in their ceremony. In the intervening 42 years it has become very popular, especially in civil wedding ceremonies.

FUNERAL

This is not a 'handbook' on how to do funerals. However, some general axioms are always worth remembering. For instance,

- A funeral will be better prepared, and those close to the deceased will be in better shape, if there is a 'breathing space' of up to a week or so between the death and the funeral.
- There should not have to be a choice between jubilant celebration and mournful misery; the fact is that someone is no longer with us, and death is final – but there *are* resources other than 'denial'.
- The distinction between funeral and wake can blur when eulogies are too many, too anecdotal (even flippant) and too long.

At many funerals, perhaps 15 percent will be regular churchgoers; 85 percent may range from those with some residue of affection for the religious content to those who feel totally out of place! In a religiously pluralist society, among the last-mentioned there may be members of other faiths. Given that the purpose of a funeral is to help people deal with the reality of loss and grief and to say their 'good-byes' to the deceased, sensitivity should be at a premium.

What follows is an outline of essentials in what I recommend the bereaved to consider – which would include a simple printed order, to obviate confusion among those who have not been in a church since the last funeral! If hymns are chosen, it is courteous for words to be printed in the order – especially if the deceased or family preferred some to be omitted! This is a funeral – **not** a memorial service.

The Meaning of the Funeral

We have gathered

- to acknowledge the uniquely special person that ...... was
- To signify our gratitude for his/her life and what he/she meant to us
- To recognise that the life force in him/her has returned to its source

- To draw consolation from a treasury of memories, from the bonds of family and friendship, from our 'faith' in whatever terms we express that.

Prayer

Eternal One, who conceived and gave birth to the cosmos, who sustains it in being and who guides it to its ultimate fulfilment, we acknowledge you as the giver of our lives and as the final claimant on us. Let us today hear the Voice that keeps alive faith and hope and love, and guides us to a good end in you. This is our prayer. Amen.

Scriptures

(suggestions only)

Psalm 139:1-6, 13-18	*Nothing is ever apart from God*
Luke 11:1-4	*The best basis of spirituality*
Philippians 4:4, 8-9	*We are as we think*

Eulogies

(up to three, but ideally not exceeding 4-5 minutes each, and scripted)

Homily

(should contain some of the following, plus links to scripture)

Grief is the normal, natural and appropriate response to loss. The intensity of it is proportional to the size of the loss. The bigger the loss, the greater the grief. The severity of the loss is proportional to the importance someone has for us.

Therefore never make light of loss and grief, nor be ashamed to weep, for tears may be both tribute to the one we have lost and healing for ourselves. Moving on from grief and loss is aided by a treasury of good memories, by the love and support of those nearest and dearest, and for those of religious inclination the knowledge that their loved one is in the good keeping of the One whence he/she came. May it be so for you.

Prayer

(an explanation like the following enables all to participate)

In a moment what some might call 'a prayer' and others perhaps 'an expression from the heart'. As you would realise, the term 'God' is for *me* rich with meaning – referring to the ground of all being, the sacred presence around us and within us. It will have meaning in similar terms for some of you, and for others will not. When I say what I call a 'prayer', this is not an act of imperialism by which I make you all religious the way I am. I invite you to be with me in an expression of gratitude for …… and an expression of solidarity with those nearest and dearest; that is to say, two 'prayers'. If you would make these sentiments your own, say 'Amen' at the end of each prayer. I address these words to the ground of being. First, an expression of gratitude.

Eternal One, we are glad and grateful for the life of ……

For his/her …… etc.

This is our prayer of gratitude. *(Let all the people say)* **AMEN**

Now an expression of solidarity.

Eternal One, we are in solidarity with ……, …… and …… May they find deep within themselves a spring that refreshes and sustains them. May they be held up by a treasury of good memories and by the love and support of those close to them. This is our prayer of solidarity with them. *(Let all the people say)* **AMEN**

Committal

The earthly life of …… is over. With great reverence we commit his/her body to the elements/ground. Earth to earth, dust to dust, but the life force returns to its origin. *(name of deceased),* rest in peace.

QUESTIONS FOR THOUGHT AND TALK

1. Here's one of those 'how long is a piece of string?' questions!
   How far do you feel we can reasonably go with modifying
   these so-called 'rites of passage' before they are no longer
   'Christian'?

2. Do you think churches and ministers generally are sensitive to
   what might be called the 'pastoral opportunities' or even (spare
   us!) the 'evangelistic opportunities' in rites of passage?

Conclusion

Worship comes from Anglo-Saxon words meaning 'worth-ship'; this implies that anything worshipped is invested with great, or even 'ultimate' worth by the worshipper.

And so, worship could be defined as the focus of undivided attention by an individual or a group on something or someone of ultimate worth. Commonly this is said to be 'God'. Paul Tillich gave us the term 'ultimate concern'.

What is commonly called 'worship' in most religious traditions may or may not fit this definition. Unfortunately, rather too often in my judgement it does not. So-called 'worship services' are frequently banal, dull and tiresome. I came home close to tears one Sunday morning and wrote in large print on my desk pad the words 'slack, disorderly and unworthy of God'!

It may be that there is a correlation between declining interest in organised religion and the style and content of worship services. I have to acknowledge that I derive little enlightenment or inspiration from some of them.

And yet, I am convinced that a basic human need is for opportunities to worship, in the purest form this can take.

Worship is both a rational and a non-rational (not 'irrational') disposition. It is similar to what one is aware of in looking at something beautiful or hearing beautiful sounds. On a recent early morning walk I stopped in my tracks at a chorus of magpies overhead. On another morning I encountered two wild ducks fossicking in the grass. When I paused and began speaking softly, one approached me to investigate, while the other kept a distance.

Worship is being aware of something beyond the immediacy of sight, hearing, touch and smell – although this awareness may well come from seeing, hearing, touching or smelling something that points beyond itself – as does an icon.

Worship in its purest form is the awareness of that surrounding, saturating sacred presence in whom dwells everything and everyone, who indwells everything and everyone, who envelops and infuses all that is. For God is in all and all is in God.

However we go about designing a liturgical event, this must be what it is all about.

APPENDIX

Following is an inventory of hymns chosen according to the seasons of the church year for a congregation in Melbourne. I am indebted to Dr Lorraine Parkinson, at the time its minister, for compiling the list and allowing its inclusion here.

ABBREVIATIONS:

IECS = *In Every Corner, Sing* (Shirley Murray)
SANS = *Sing a New Song* (George Stuart)
CG = *Common Ground'* (John Bell Ed.)
GWPY = *God, We Praise You* (Keith Pearson)
Where hymns have no abbreviation, they are from *Together in Song*

N.B.
Eucharist hymns are in **bold**.
Baptism hymns are <u>underlined</u>.
Tunes included are those used instead of set tunes.

EPIPHANY

447 'Lord, your almighty word'
707 'Bread is blessed and broken'
111 'Praise to the Lord'
417 – 'Loving Spirit' *Omnie Die* 101
IECS66 – 'Take my gifts and let me love you' *Blaenwern* 590
188 – 'Where wide sky rolls down' *Laudate Dominum* 215
668 – 'Touch the earth lightly' *Bunessan* 156
148 – 'All things praise you, Lord most high'
117 – 'The Lord Jehovah reigns'
SANS4 – 'It is so grand' *Woodlands*
SANS13 – 'All creation sings a story' *Praise my soul*
SANS15 – 'God's Love Gives Freedom' *Blaenwern*
476 – 'As a chalice cast of gold' *Dix* 314
420 – 'Holy Spirit, go before us' *Hyfrydol* 217(i)

161 – 'Tell out, my soul'

61 – 'Sing, all creation' *Christe Sanctorum* (1) 472

598 – 'Dear Father, Lord of humankind' *Rest* MHB AT23

507 – 'Come, Spirit blest'

TRANSFIGURATION

102 – 'Praise to the living God'

152 – 'Joyful, joyful, we adore you'

165 – 'Praise our God, the great Creator'

LENT

47 – 'Our God, our help in ages past'

444 – 'Dear Shepherd of your people, hear' *Belmont* 514

CG145 – 'When our confidence is shaken' *Westminster Abbey*

560(ii) – 'All my hope on God is founded' *Meine Hoffnung*

59 – 'All people that on earth do dwell'

190 – 'Colourful Creator, God of mystery *Au clair de la lune* 236

691 – 'Faith will not grow from words alone'

585 – 'I heard the voice of Jesus say'

593 – 'Lord, take my hand and lead me'

506 – 'Author of life divine'

577 – ' Come, let us to the Lord our God'

CG78 – 'Lord, we come to ask your healing' *Ar hyd y nos* 168

683 – 'God! When human bonds are broken' *Omnie Die* 101

201 – 'King of glory, King of peace'

130 – 'We plough the fields and scatter'

76 – 'I to the hills will lift my eyes'

CG8 – 'As a fire is meant for burning' *Blaenwern* 590

PALM SUNDAY

IECS3 – 'Celebrate each generation' *Stuttgart* 272

CG117 – 'Spirit of God, unseen as the wind'

GOOD FRIDAY

339 – 'O sacred head sore wounded'

IECS67 – 'Teach us, O loving heart of Christ' *Amazing Grace* 129

342 – 'When I survey the wondrous cross'

EASTER DAY

156 – 'Morning has broken'

394 – 'Christ is risen! Shout Hosanna!' *Hyfrydol* 217

523 – 'Here, Lord, we take the broken bread'

SANS39 – 'Strong love' *Austria*

EASTER

154 – 'Great is your faithfulness, O God my Father'

CG141 – 'What shall we pray for those who died' **(For Anzac Day)**

672 – 'Lord of earth and all creation' *Westminster Abbey*

126 – 'God moves in a mysterious way'

648 – 'Help us accept each other' *Crüger* 202

CG98 – 'One bread, one body'

153 – 'God is love, let heav'n adore him'

IECS11 – 'Come, celebrate the women' *Ellacombe* (2)

161 – 'Tell out, my soul'

588 – 'In heavenly love abiding'

GWPY 7 (Pearson) 'God is truly present' *Wunderbarer König* 121

104 – 'While morning still is breaking' *Ellacombe* (1) 361

631 – 'Father, Lord of all creation' *Hyfrydol* 217(i)

ASCENSION

557 – 'All things praise you'

184 – 'When trouble strikes and fear takes root' *Rockingham* 342

653 – 'This is a day of new beginnings' vv. 1-4 *St Clement* 458

179 – 'Praise with joy the world's Creator'

PENTECOST

415 – 'Praise the spirit in creation' *Westminster Abbey* 432

TRINITY

626 – 'Lord of creation, to you be all praise!'

453 – 'We limit not the truth of God'
429 – 'Break now the bread of life'

SEASON OF PENTECOST
44 – 'How lovely is your dwelling place'
550 – 'Our Father, God in heaven above' *Melita* 138
409 – 'O breath of life, come sweeping through us'
107 – 'Sing praise and thanksgiving'
692 – 'Sometimes a healing word is comfort' *Neumark* 554
CG45 – 'Great God, your love has called us here' *Melita*138
564 – 'O God of Bethel'
699 – 'A new commandment'
613 – 'Lord of all hopefulness'
CG138 – 'We cannot measure how you heal' *Ye banks and braes*
593 – 'Lord, take my hand and lead me'
CG148 – 'Will you come and follow me'
599(ii) – 'Take my life and let it be' *Nottingham*
470 – 'Rejoice in God's saints' *Laudate Dominum* 96
SANS56 – 'Fruits of the Spirit' *St Agnes*
SANS59 – 'Questions' *Love Divine* 217(ii)
SANS61 – 'Moving Forward in Belief' *Stuttgart*
SANS76 – 'That joyous day' *Irish*
SANS81 – 'Sacred Writings?' *Ellacombe* (2)
SANS100 – 'Our Mother Earth' *Nun Danket*
SANS102 – 'More than tolerance' *Austria*
627 – 'Praise and thanksgiving'
625 – 'I need you, Lord'
SANS38 – 'Jesus – the Revealer' *Chilton Foliat* 487
158 – 'God has spoken by his prophets' *Austria* 93
621 – 'O God of every nation' *Aurelia* 457
187 – 'Let all creation dance'
430 – 'Your words to me are life and health'
553 – 'In all my ways, in every task'
90 – 'I'll praise my maker while I've breath'
577 – 'Come, let us to the Lord our God'

607 – 'Make me a channel of your peace'

CG29 – 'When I receive the peace of Christ' *Ellacombe* (2) 453

448 – 'Blest are the pure in heart'

638 – 'O Christ, the healer, we have come' *Herongate* 488

CG35 – 'For your generous providing' *Blaenwern* 590

154 – 'Great is your faithfulness'

111 – 'Praise to the Lord'

161 – 'Tell out, my soul'

437 – 'Blessèd Jesus, at your word'

589 – 'Jesus calls us! O'er the tumult'

635 – 'Forgive our sins as we forgive' *St Bernard* 459(ii)

152 – 'Joyful, joyful, we adore you' *Hyfrydol* 217(i)

106 – 'Now thank we all our God'

167 – 'How deep the riches of our God' *St Peter* 485

96 – 'Sing praise to the Lord'

460 'The call of God' *Aurelia* 457

117 – 'The Lord Jehovah reigns'

144 – 'Lord, you have been our dwelling place'

CG93 – 'O God, you are my God alone'

201 – 'King of glory, King of peace'

680 – 'God! As with silent hearts' *Eventide* 586

621 – 'O God of every nation' *Aurelia* 457

274 – 'The people that in darkness walked'

IECS36 – 'Great God of earth and heaven' *Aurelia* 457

416 – 'Great God, your Spirit like the wind'

CG74 – 'Lord, for the years your love has … ' *Tree of Peace* AHB503(ii)

569 – 'Guide me, O thou great Redeemer'

561 – 'Who would true valour see'

15 – 'God is my strong salvation;

555 – 'Put all your trust in God' *Diademata* 228

121 – 'God himself is present'

288 – 'Not the powerful, not the privileged'

83 – 'Let us with a gladsome mind'

559 – 'A new heart, Lord, create in me' *Rivaulx* 131

110 – 'Sing praise to God who reigns above' *Mit Freuden Zart* 479

673 – 'I set the Lord before my eyes' *Luther* 144

SANS50 – 'All will be well' *To God be the glory* 147

143 – 'Immortal, invisible'

REIGN OF CHRIST

679 – 'God of Jeremiah'

CG49 – 'Heaven shall not wait'

ADVENT

275 – 'Hail to the Lord's anointed'

690 – 'Beauty for brokenness'

CG148 – 'Will you come and follow me'

538 – 'Feed us now, bread of life'

688 – 'Come to be our hope, O Jesus' *Blaenwern* 590

<u>490 – 'Lord Jesus, once a child'</u>

274 – 'The people that in darkness walked'

284 – 'O bless the God of Israel' *Crüger* 275

CHRISTMAS

324 – 'Lord, bid your servant go in peace'

291 – 'Earth has many a noble city'

IECS39 – 'Here to the house of God we come' *Melita* 138

BIBLIOGRAPHY

Beauregard, Mario, and Denyse O'Leary. *The Spiritual Brain: A Neuroscientists's Case for the Existence of the Soul.* New York: Harper Collins, 2008.

Bodycomb, John. *Excited to Speak, Exciting to Hear.* Adelaide: Open Book, 2003

Bodycomb, John. *No Fixed Address: Faith as Journey.* Melbourne: Spectrum Publications Pty Ltd., 2010.

Clynes, Manfred. *Sentics: The Touch of the Emotions.* Lindfield NSW, Unity Press, 1989.

Grainger, Roger. *The Drama of the Rite: Worship, Liturgy & Theatre Performance.* Sussex Academic Press, 2008.

Jamison, Abbot Christopher. *Finding Sanctuary: Monastic Steps for Everyday Life.* London: Weidenfeld & Nicolson, 2006.

Macnab, Francis. *A Fine Wind is Blowing.* Melbourne: Spectrum Publications, 2003.

McNamara, Patrick. *The Neuroscience of Religious Experience.* New York, NY: Cambridge University Press, 2009.

Morwood, Michael. *Praying a New Story.* Melbourne: Spectrum Publications, 2003.

Newberg, Andrew. *The Mystical Mind: Probing the Biology of Religious Experience.* Augsburg Fortress Press, 1999

Newberg, Andrew. *Why God Won't Go Away: Brain Science and the Biology of Belief.* Ballantine, 2002.

Newberg, Andrew, with Mark Robert Waldman. *Why we Believe What We Believe: Uncovering our Biological Need for Meaning, Spirituality and Truth.* Free Press, 2006

Otto, Rudolf. *The Idea of the Holy.* Oxford University, 1950.

Parkinson, Lorraine. *The World According to Jesus: His Blueprint for the Best Possible World.* Melbourne: Spectrum Publications Pty Ltd., 2011.

Sim, Stuart. *Manifesto for Silence: Confronting the Politics and Culture of Noise.* Edinburgh: Edinburgh University Press, 2007.

Spong, John Shelby. *The Sins of Scripture: Exposing the Bible's Texts of Hate to Reveal the Love of God*. San Francisco: HarperCollins, 2005.

Steele, Bruce. *Music & The Church*. Bell Tower Publications (St Aidan's Uniting Church, North Balwyn), 2004.

Steele, Bruce. *Singing the Psalms in the Twenty-first Century*. Bell Tower, 2005.

Underhill, Evelyn. *Worship*. London: Nisbet & Co, 1936

White, James. *Introduction to Christian Worship*. Nashville, Tenn.: Abingdon, 1981

Wuthnow, Robert. *Creative Spirituality: The Way of the Artist*. Los Angeles: University of California Press. 2001.

Wuthnow, Robert. *All in Sync: How Music and Art are Revitalizing American Religion*. Los Angeles: University of California Press. 2003.

AND NOT TO BE MISSED!

A splendid source of material, generously shared by
Rex Hunt, can be fished via his web site:
www.rexaehuntprogressive.com

Made in the USA
Las Vegas, NV
12 January 2021

15717410R00075